JN099721

経済の基礎も英語も学べる!

新版 英語対訳で読む「経済」入門

大島朋剛
Tomotaka Oshima 監修

Elizabeth Mills
英文監訳

j JIPPI
Compact

実業之日本社

Our daily life is closely related to the economy. We work to earn money and live our lives spending it on commodities and services. We pay taxes and receive government services and also take out various insurances provided by the government for protection. All of these are parts of the economy. However, there might be many people who are not interested in this.

This book explains the basic structure of the economy and a brief history both in English and Japanese. The English phrases are written to be read from the beginning to the end.

Recently, we can easily find and read economic news written in English if you use the internet. The English economic articles, which are written from a different viewpoint, are beneficial to understand the movement of the world economy, whatever business you are engaged in.

The articles of this book cover the concepts and words which are necessary to understand the economy in English. You will be able to read the English newspaper or website articles without struggle, if you learn these concepts and words.

We hope this book will help you to read and understand economic articles written in English.

私たちの日常生活は、深く経済と結びついています。私たちは、働いてお金を稼ぎ、そのお金を使いながらモノやサービスを購入・消費して生活しています。国に税金を支払って国のサービスを受け、公的保険制度に加入して保障を受けます。これらすべては、経済活動の一部です。にも関わらず、そうした経済のことに関心がない人が意外に多いのではないでしょうか。

　この本は、経済の基本的なしくみや用語、大まかな歴史を、日本語と英語で解説しています。英文は、頭からどんどん読んで理解できるように配慮されています。

　現在は、英語で書かれた内外の経済情報を、手軽にインターネットで読むことができます。日本語の報道とは異なる視点で書かれた海外の経済の情報を読み取り、世界経済の動きを把握することは、どんな仕事をしている人にも有益なことです。

　本書は、英語で経済を理解するうえで必要な単語を網羅しています。これらを覚えることで、英字新聞やWEBに英語で書かれた記事に、抵抗なく入っていけるようになります。

　本書が、英語で書かれた経済ニュースを読む一助となれば、幸いです。

[本書の効果的な使い方]
本書の英文の下に書かれてある日本語訳は、100円ショップや文房具店で市販されている透明の赤シート（暗記シート）をあてると見えなくなります。英文だけを読みたいときや、単語の暗記をするときには、赤シートをご購入のうえ、ご利用ください。

CONTENTS / 目次

CONTENTS / 目次

Chapter 6

History of Japanese Economy/ 日本経済の歴史

CONTENTS / 目次

装幀	杉本 欣右
イラスト	笹森 識
日本文執筆	森井 美紀
英文執筆	中村 英良
経済監修協力	高橋 伴往（金融）
	牧内 勝哉（財政）
英文監訳協力	Jared Kettler（金融・経済）
DTP・編集	スタジオスパーク

Chapter **1**

Fundamental
Japanese Economy

第 1 章

日本経済の基本

INTRODUCTION TO THE ECONOMY

1. What Is Economy?

①Can you answer the question <u>immediately</u> "what is
すぐに
economy?" ②In a few words, economy is an <u>activity</u>
経済   活動
associated with the giving and receiving of money. ③<u>Trading</u>
〜に関連した   取り引きすること
<u>tangible</u> things or services for money is called "<u>object</u>
形のある   実物経済
<u>economy</u>". ④We use money to buy things and to <u>obtain</u>
受ける
services in our <u>daily lives</u>. ⑤We buy <u>snacks</u> at <u>convenience</u>
日常生活   スナック菓子   コンビニ
<u>stores</u>, eat lunch in restaurants, and get haircuts at <u>the barber</u>
理髪店
<u>shop</u>. ⑥All of these are examples of object economy.

⑦Money, <u>originally</u> a <u>medium</u> for trading things, is often
本来は   媒介
traded as a <u>commodity</u>. ⑧Economic activity without
商品
tangible things or services is called "<u>monetary economy</u>".
マネー経済
⑨We <u>might</u> <u>save</u> money in a <u>bank account</u>, buy <u>stocks</u> from
かもしれない 貯金する   銀行口座   株
a <u>broker</u> or <u>take out</u> a <u>life insurance policy</u>. ⑩These
証券会社   (保険に)入る 生命保険契約
<u>activities</u> are examples of monetary economy. ⑪In object
行動
economy, commodities <u>are traded for</u> money which has the
〜と交換される
same <u>value</u>. ⑫<u>On the other hand</u>, in monetary economy,
価値   一方で
money itself <u>is treated as</u> the commodity.
〜として扱われる

⑬Monetary economy rapidly expanded in size after the year 2000.

急激に　拡大した

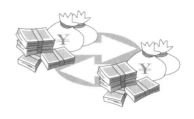

1. 経済とは？

①「経済とは何？」とたずねられたら、あなたはすぐに答えられますか？　②ひと言でいうならば、**経済とはお金のやりとりに関わる活動**のことです。③形のあるモノや、販売されているサービスに対してお金を払うことを「**実物経済**」といいます。④私たちは普段の生活でモノを買い、受けたサービスに対してお金を払います。⑤私たちは、コンビニでお菓子を買い、レストランでランチを食べ、理髪店で髪を切ってもらいます。⑥これが実物経済です。

⑦本来、貨幣はモノの取り引きをするときの媒介でしたが、貨幣自体が商品として取り引きされることもあります。⑧モノやサービスが介在しない経済活動を「**マネー経済**」といいます。⑨お金を銀行に預けたり、証券会社を通して株を買ったり、生命保険に入ったりするでしょう。⑩それがマネー経済です。⑪実物経済では、お金は同等の価値を持ったモノと交換されます。⑫一方、マネー経済では、お金自体が商品として扱われます。⑬2000年以降、マネー経済の規模が飛躍的に拡大しています。

2. Three Economic Units

①Economic activities are carried out by three units: households, companies and government.
②Companies produce goods or services using labor, land and capital. ③They profit by selling the products while paying wages to the workers, interest for capital and rent for land.
④Companies sometimes use their profits to develop capital investment for productive activities.
⑤Households earn income by providing labor to a corporation while consuming products and services.
⑥Surplus money could be saved in the bank.
⑦The government supplies services which individuals or companies cannot provide. ⑧They use taxes collected from households and companies to supply various services such as police and fire department, social security, as well as building infrastructures such as bridges and roads. ⑨These three units are closely related and affect each other. ⑩If a company is not performing well, household incomes will decrease, and the

financial condition of the government will weaken.
財政状況　　　　　　　　　　　　　　　　　　　減退する

2. 経済の3つの主体

①経済活動を行なう主体は**企業**、**家計**、**政府**の3つです。

②企業は、労働力、土地、資本を使って商品やサービスを生産します。③これを売ることで利潤を得て、労働力には賃金、資本には利子、土地には地代を払います。④企業は生産活動のための設備投資にあてることもあります。

⑤家計は労働力を企業に提供して生産活動をし、その対価として給与や報酬を得て、モノやサービスを購入・消費します。⑥余ったお金は銀行に預けたりします。

⑦家計や企業では提供できない公共サービスを扱うのが政府です。⑧企業や家計から徴収した税金を使い、社会保障や、警察、消防などさまざまな行政サービスを提供したり、道路や橋の建設といったインフラの整備を行なったりします。

⑨この企業、家計、政府は、相互に密接な関係にあります。⑩企業の業績が振るわなければ、家計の収入が減り、政府の財政は悪化します。

3. Microeconomics And Macroeconomics

①Economics can be divided into two fields: microeconomics
経済学　　　　　　　　　～に分けられる　　　　　　　　ミクロ経済学

and macroeconomics. ②Microeconomics is the branch that
マクロ経済学　　　　　　　　　　　　　　　　　　　　部門

analyzes the economic activities of individuals and
分析する　　　　経済行為　　　　　　　　　　　　個人

companies. ③Meanwhile, macroeconomics is the branch that
企業　　　　　一方

analyzes the comprehensive economy from a broader
　　　　　　総合的な　　　　　　　　　　　　広い

perspective; for example the movement of money in a
視点

country. ④Microeconomics is a system in which prices are

determined in the selling and buying by companies or
決まる

households. ⑤On this basis, it figures out how inflation or
家計　　　　これを基に　　　判断する　　　　　インフレ

deflation influences the production activities of companies
デフレ　　　影響を与える　生産活動

or household consumption. ⑥Macroeconomics studies the
家計消費　　　　　　　　　　　　　　　　調べる

three entities: government, companies and households, from
主体　　　政府

a broad perspective. ⑦It analyzes the economy with

statistical data such as GDP, the national income and
統計資料　　　　　　　　　　　　　　国民所得

economic indicators, and predicts the future economic
指数　　　　予測する

conditions such as inflation and deflation. ⑧Macroeconomics
状態

is important for the government in order to introduce
導入する

effective policies.
効果的な

⑨British economist, Keynes (see p.86) thought that the
ケインズ
market doctrine, which is based only on the free economic
市場原理 もとづく
activities of people, was not entirely to be trusted.
完全に
⑩Macroeconomics was developed on this idea.

3. ミクロ経済学とマクロ経済学

①経済学には、**ミクロ経済学**と**マクロ経済学**があります。②個人や企業の経済活動を分析するのがミクロ経済学です。③一方、国のなかのお金の動きなど、全体的な視点から経済を分析するのがマクロ経済学です。④ミクロ経済学の対象の中心となるのは、企業や家計がモノを売り買いするなかで、価格が決められるしくみです。⑤そのうえで、インフレやデフレが企業の生産活動や家計の消費にどのような影響を与えるのかといったことを、明らかにしていきます。⑥マクロ経済学は、政府、企業、家計という3つの経済主体を、広い視野に立って分析していきます。⑦GDP、国民所得、景気指数といったデータをもとにして、経済の状態を分析し、将来のデフレ、インフレといった経済状態を予測します。⑧これは、有効な経済政策をとるうえで重要です。
⑨イギリスの経済学者・ケインズ（p.86参照）は、国民の自由な経済活動のみに基づく市場原理（競争原理）を完全に信頼することはできないと考えました。⑩マクロ経済学は、この考え方をもとに発展してきました。

4. Market

①The place where goods and services are traded is a market.
モノ　　サービス

②In economics, various forms of market are envisioned. ③In
経済学では　　　　　形　　　　　　想定される

the agricultural market trade, for example, carrots where there
農産物の

are many buyers and sellers, one buyer or seller do not have an
買い手　　売り手

affect on the market price. ④It is a competitive market. ⑤On
影響　市場価格　　　　　　　　　　　競争市場

the other hand, in an area where we cannot watch television
一方で　　　　地域

unless we make a contract with a cable company, the price is
〜でない限り　　契約

determined by only one seller. ⑥This is a monopoly market.
決められる　　　　　　　　　　　独占市場

⑦Additionally, in the beer and mobile phone markets in Japan,
また　　　　　　　　　　携帯電話

there is not a strong price competition. ⑧This is an
厳しい価格競争

oligopoly.
寡占

⑨In the perfect competition market, where every participant
完全競争市場　　　　　　　　　　　　　参加者

accepts the price as given, if the demand is increasing, the
受け入れる　　与えられたものとして　需要　　　多くなる

price rises up to the point at which the seller accepts it. ⑩In
〜まで上がる　　　　　　　　　　　　　受け入れる

contrast, if the supply is increasing, the price goes down to the
対照的に(→反対に)　供給

point at which the buyer accepts it. ⑪As the price of a
〜につれて

commodity becomes higher, the manufacturers produce
製造業者(→売り手)　　生産する

more. ⑫<u>Once</u> the supply <u>exceeds</u> the demand, the price begins
　　　いったん〜すると　　　　超える
to go down and the demand begins to increase. ⑬<u>Accordingly</u>,
　　　　　　　　　　　　　　　　　　　　　　　　　　　　　　それに応じて
<u>the market price</u> is determined at the point where supply and
市場価格
demand <u>are balanced</u>.
　　　　　均衡する（つり合う）

4. 市場

①モノ・サービスを売買する場が「市場（しじょう）」です。②経済学では、さまざまな形態の市場が想定されます。③たとえばニンジンなどの農産物の市場には、多くの買い手と売り手が存在し、1人の売り手や買い手は市場価格に影響をおよぼしません。④これが**競争市場**です。⑤他方、ケーブルテレビ局1社と契約しなければテレビを見られない地域では、1つの売り手が販売価格を決めます。⑥これが**独占市場**です。⑦また、日本のビールや携帯電話のように、売り手が少数しか存在せず、販売価格であまり厳しい競争をしていない市場もあります。⑧これを**寡占（かせん）**といいます。

⑨市場への参加者が価格を所与（しょよ）として受け入れる**完全競争市場**では、需要が高まれば、売り手が納得するところまで価格が上がります。⑩反対に、供給が多くなれば、買い手が納得するところまで価格が下がります。⑪価格が上昇するにつれ、売り手は増産を進めます。⑫しかし供給が需要を上回るようになると、今度は価格が下がり始めるとともに、需要が増大します。⑬そして、**市場価格**が決まったところが、**需要と供給の均衡点**となります。

5. Invisible Hand

①"Invisible hand" is a term which Adam Smith used in "The
見えざる手　　　　　　　言葉

Wealth of Nations" published in 1776. ②This term is often
『国富論』

used to briefly explain the system of a market economy.
簡潔に　説明する　しくみ　　市場経済

③The term which appears in "The Wealth of Nations" is
登場する

summarized as follows: In a market economy, although
要約される　　　　以下のように　　　　　　　　　　　　　　　　　　　～にも関わらず

individuals are concerned only with their own profits,
個人　　　　～だけに関心がある　　　　　　　　　　　利益

the end result of their economic activity increases the
最終的な結果　　　　　　　経済活動

profits of society as though involuntarily led by an
社会　　　　まるで～のように　無意識に　　～によって導かれる

"invisible hand".

④The term, "invisible hand" implies that the power of God is
ほのめかす

controlling the market adjustment mechanism.
市場調整機能

⑤In "The Theory of Moral Sentiments" published prior to
『道徳感情論』　　　　　　　　　　　出版された　～に先立って

"The Wealth of Nations", Smith mentioned that all actions
～と述べた

should be fair even if it is done for the profit of an individual.
個人の利益

⑥This means that it is important to put oneself in the position
意味する　　　　　　　　　　　　　　　　　　　　　　立場

of others in order to make society prosperous.
～させる　　繁栄している

⑦The term "invisible hand" often indicates a mechanism
示す　　　しくみ

in which the market price is automatically adjusted.
自動的に　　　調整された

⑧Economists often refer to this term to make the argument
経済学者(エコノミスト)　～を述べる　　　議論する

that the government should not interfere with the market.
干渉する

5. 見えざる手

①「見えざる手」とは、1776年に発行された**アダム・スミス**の『**国富論**』のなかに出てくる言葉です。②この言葉は、市場経済のしくみを簡潔に説明する場合に、よく使われます。③『国富論』のその部分を要約すると「経済活動においては、自己の富を増やそうとする諸個人は、**見えざる手**に導かれ、意図せずして社会の利益を増大させる」とあります。

④「見えざる手」は、暗に神によって市場調整機能が働いていることを意味します。

⑤スミスは、『国富論』に先立って書いた『道徳感情論』のなかで、個人の利益のための行為に対しても、フェアプレイが守られるべきだと説いています。⑥社会を繁栄させるために、相手の立場になって考えることが重要だということです。

⑦「見えざる手」は、市場によって自動的に価格が決定されるしくみを指すことがあります。⑧時として、経済の専門家はこの言葉を引き合いに出して、「政府は経済に介入すべきではない」と主張します。

6. Economic Conditions

①We often see the phrase "economic conditions are bad" in
経済の状況（→景気）

newspapers. ②What does this phrase mean? ③If you are

working at a company, you might realize that economic
～かもしれない 自覚する

conditions are not good when you take a pay cut. ④A
賃金カット

company might notice it when sales are weak and revenue
気がつく　　　　　売上高　　　　　　　　収入

begins to decrease. ⑤Once economic conditions become
減少する

worse, companies hold back on recruitment and scale down
～を控える　　　採用　　　　　～を縮小する

operations. ⑥Companies' earnings decrease, employee
事業　　　　　　　　　　　　　収益　　　減少する　従業員の

wages are cut, and the number of jobless people increases.
賃金　　　　　　～の数　　　　　　　　　　　　　増加する

⑦As a result, the government, with the expectation of a
その結果　　　　　　　　　　　　　　予期

reduced tax revenue, would need to issue a deficit bond.
減少した　税収　　　　　　　　　　　　発行する 赤字国債

⑧When economic conditions improve, the performance of
よくなる　　業績

companies also improve and employee salaries rise.
給料

⑨People purchase more things and companies increase their
購入する

performance even more. ⑩Employee salaries also increase.
業績

⑪Subsequently, a greater amount of money circulates in the
続いて　　　　　　大量の　　　　　　　　　　循環する

economy, which boosts economic activity.
持ち上げる（→活性化する）

20

⑫Therefore government tax revenues increase and financial
　　　　その結果　　　政府の税収　　　　　　　　　　　　　　財政赤字
deficits decrease.

6. 景気

①新聞を読むと、よく「景気が悪い（不況）」という表現を見かけます。②これは、いったいどういう意味でしょうか？　③会社勤めをしている人なら、給料が下がると「景気が悪くなった」と感じるでしょう。④企業なら、売り上げが下がり、収益が減ると、「景気が悪い」と感じるはずです。⑤一度、景気が悪くなると、会社は雇用を控え、事業を縮小します。⑥会社の収益が減り、従業員の給料が削減され、失業者の数が増えます。⑦その結果、政府の税収が減ると予期されるので、赤字国債の発行を迫られることにもなります。

⑧「景気がよい（好景気・好況）」ときは、会社は業績を伸ばし、従業員の給料が上がります。⑨人の購買力が高まり、会社はさらに業績を伸ばします。⑩すると、従業員の給料もさらに上がります。⑪たくさんのお金が社会で動き、経済活動を活性化します。⑫こうして政府の税収は増え、財政赤字が減少します。

7. Business Cycles

①In a capitalist economy, periodic expansion and
資本主義経済　　　　　周期的な　拡張
contraction of economic activity is repeated. ②This is called the
収縮
"business cycle". ③There are a variety of business cycle
景気循環　　　　　　　いろいろな
models: Kitchin inventory, Juglar fixed investment,
キチンの在庫(→キチンの波)　ジュグラーの固定投資　(→ジュグラーの波)
Kuznets infrastructual investment and Kondratiev
クズネッツのインフラ投資(→クズネックの波)　　　　　コンドラチェフの波
wave. ④In the actual economy, these models are combined to
実際の　　　　　　　　　　　組み合わされて
form a complex wave-shape.
複雑な

⑤The most well known model among them is "Kitchin
inventory", proposed by economist Joseph Kitchin in the
提唱された
1920s. ⑥His model explains the movement of economic
説明する
activity with the changing of inventory. ⑦The process of the
在庫　　　　　　過程
cycle is as follows: rise of economic conditions, decrease of
周期　　　　　　　　　　　上昇　景気　　　　　　　減少
inventory, expansion of production, a cyclical peak,
拡大　　　　　　　　　　循環の
recession, decrease of shipments, increase of inventory,
景気後退　　　　　　出荷
reduction of production, a cyclical bottom, restart of
減少　　　　　　　　　　　景気の底　　　　　再開
production and upturn in business. ⑧The Kitchin inventory,
好転
which has a comparatively short cycle, takes about 40
比較的　　　　　　　　　　　　　　かかる

months. ⑨The model which has the longest cycle, is the Kondratiev wave. ⑩This wave is caused by a historical
<u>～によって生じる</u>　　　<u>歴史的な</u>
event such as revolution, war or innovation in technology.
<u>革命</u>　　　　　　　<u>技術革新</u>
⑪The Kondratiev wave precipitated cycle takes about 50 to
<u>引き起こされた</u>
70 years.

7. 景気循環

①資本主義経済下では経済活動の拡張と収縮が繰り返されます。②これは**景気循環**と呼ばれています。③景気循環には、**キチンの波、ジュグラーの波、クズネッツの波、コンドラチェフの波**などのモデルがあります。④実際の経済では、これらの波が一体化し、複雑な波を形成しています。

⑤これらのなかでもっとも知られてきたのは、1920年代の経済学者、ジョゼフ・キチンが提唱したキチンの波（在庫循環の波）です。⑥キチンのモデルでは、経済の活動の変化を製品の在庫量の変化によって説明しています。⑦周期は以下の順に変化します。景気の上昇→在庫の減少→生産の拡大→景気のピーク→景気後退→出荷の減少→在庫の増加→生産の縮小→景気の底→生産再開による景気の好転。⑧キチンの波は、比較的短く、1周期は約40カ月です。⑨これらのモデルのなかでもっとも長い周期を持つのは、コンドラチェフの波です。⑩これは、革命や戦争、技術革新といった歴史的な出来事によって生まれます。⑪コンドラチェフの波の1周期は約50～70年です。

8. Gross Domestic Product (GDP)

①Gross Domestic Product (GDP) is one of the economic
総計の　　　国内の　　　　生産物　　　　国内総生産

indexes which indicates the size of the economy of a country.
指標　　　　　　示す

②It is the amount of goods and services produced
総額

domestically and traded in the market in one year. ③GDP
国内で　　　　　　取引された

can be calculated by summing up the added-value of all
計算された　　　合計すること　　付加価値

industrial sectors. ④Added-value is the difference between
産業部門　　　　　　　　　　　　　差

the price of materials plus fuel and the products which are
材料　　　　燃料　　　　製品

produced.

⑤Let us take *udon* noodles as an example. ⑥Wheat is
うどん　　　　　　　例　　　　　　小麦

produced by farms, milled by flour mills, processed into
農家　　　粉にされた　　製粉業者　　加工された

udon noodles by noodle companies, and served in *udon*
製麺会社　　　　　　　　　提供された

restaurants as a meal. ⑦Value is added at each stage in this
価値

process. ⑧When we calculate the GDP in this way, only the

added-values are totaled up in order to avoid duplicating
合計された　　　　　　　避ける　重複すること

the material costs.

⑨GDP calculated as the total of added-value as noted
上記のように

above is called "GDP estimated by production approach".
推計された　　生産面

8.GDP（国内総生産）

①国の経済の規模を表す目安に、**GDP（国内総生産）**があります。②1年間に国内で生産され、市場で取引されたモノ・サービスの金額の総額です。③GDPの算出は、各産業でつけられた**付加価値**を合計するという方法をとります。④付加価値とは、原材料や燃料などと加工された製品の価値の差です。

⑤うどんの例をみてみましょう。⑥小麦は農家によって生産され、製粉業者によって粉になり、製麺業者によってうどんに加工され、だしや具とともにうどん屋で提供されます。⑦この過程のそれぞれの段階で、価値が付加されていきます。⑧GDPの計算では、原材料費を二重計算しないようにするため、その付加価値だけを合計します。

⑨このように、付加価値の合計として算出されたGDPは、「**生産面からみたGDP**」と呼ばれます。

9. Principle of Equivalent of Three Aspects

①There are three approaches to calculate GDP: production
取り組み方　　　　　　　　　　　　生産
approach, income approach and expenditure approach.
　　　　　所得　　　　　　　　　支出

②Totaling the values added in the manufacturing processes,
　　　　　価値　　　　　　　　製造過程
as noted in the previous page, is the "GDP estimated by
　　　　　　前の　　　　　　　　　　　　推計された
production approach".

③The total income of the company and the labor related to
　　　　　　　　　　　　　　　　　　　　労働者　　　　　〜に関わった
production should be equal to the total value added in the
manufacturing process of the goods. ④Therefore, we can
　　　　　　　　　　　商品　　　　　したがって
figure out GDP by totaling all income. ⑤This method to
算出する　　　　　　　　　　　　　　　　　　　方法
calculate GDP is the "GDP estimated by income approach".

⑥If a company or an individual receives income, they spend
　　　　　　　　　　　　　　　受け取る
money. ⑦Accordingly, total expenditure is equal to GDP.
　　　　その結果
⑧This method to calculate GDP by totaling all expenses is
　　　　　　　　　　　　　　　　　　　　支出
the "GDP estimated by expenditure approach".

⑨The "principle of equivalent of three aspects" means that
原則　　　　　　等価なもの　　　　　局面(→三面等価の原則)
GDP, when calculated with all three approaches, are
equivalent.

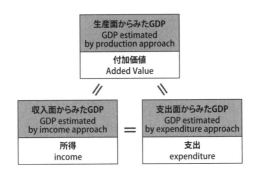

9. 三面等価の原則

①GDP は**生産、所得、支出**から算出することができます。
②前ページでも解説したように、製造過程での付加価値を合計すると GDP が得られますが、これは「**生産面からみた GDP**」です。
③製造工程に関わる企業や労働者などの収入を合計すると、商品の製造工程の付加価値と同じになります。④したがって、収入をすべて合計するという方法でも GDP を求めることができます。
⑤この方法で算出した GDP が、「**収入面からみた GDP**」です。
⑥個人も企業も収入があれば、お金を使います。⑦そこで、総支出も GDP と同じ値になります。⑧このように、すべての支出を合計して得た GDP が「**支出面からみた GDP**」です。
⑨**三面等価の原則**とは、これら３つから算出した GDP は等価になることを意味します。

10. Economic Growth Rate and Potential Growth Rate

①The rate of change of the GDP is called the "economic
　　　　　　割合
growth rate. ②The economic growth rate is calculated by
　　　　　　　経済成長率　　　　　　　　　　　　計算される
subtracting the previous year's GDP from the current
…から引き算をして　前年のGDP　　　　　　　今年(のGDP)
year's and dividing by the previous year's GDP. ③For
　　　　割り算をして
example, if the GDP of the previous year is 508 trillion yen
　　　　　　　　　　　　　　　　　　　　　　　兆
and that of this year is 510 trillion yen, the economic growth
is 0.4 % (510 trillion - 508 trillion = 2 trillion. 2 trillion / 508
trillion = 0.4%[※]). ④We should notice that, even though the
　　　　　　　　　　　　注意する　　たとえ〜としても
difference between the GDP this year and last year is two
trillion yen, the economic growth rate varies according to the
　　　　　　　　　　　　　　　　　　変化する　〜によって
size of the economy. ⑤In the beginning of the 1960s, the size
規模
of the Japanese economy was around 20 trillion yen, much
　　　　　　　　　　　　　　　　およそ　　　　　　　　ずっと
smaller than now. ⑥If the GDP of a given year in this
　　　　　　　　　　　　　　　　ある年の
period was 20 trillion yen and it increased by two trillion yen
to 22 trillion yen the next year, the economic growth rate came
to 10 %, as calculated by dividing 2 trillion by 20 trillion.

⑦Recently in Japan, as the economy has grown in size, we
近年の

　　　　※ 読み方は、Five hundred and ten trillion minus five hundred and eight trillion equals two
　　　　trillion. Two trillion divided by five hundred and eight trillion equals point four percent.

cannot expect a high economic growth rate.
期待する
⑧Three factors considered in production are capital, labor
要素　　　考えられる　　　生産において　　　　資本　　労働力
and technology. ⑨Economic growth rate would be highest
技術
when these three factors reach their potential. ⑩Growth rate
潜在力
which fulfills the potential capacity of these three factors is
発揮する　　　　　能力
called "potential growth rate".

10. 経済成長率と潜在成長率

①GDP の伸び率を「**経済成長率**」と呼びます。②1 年間に増え
た GDP の金額を前年の GDP で割って計算します。③たとえば、
前年度の GDP が508兆円で、今年度の GDP が510兆円とすると、
経済成長率は（510 − 508）÷ 508 ＝ 0.4％になります。④去年
と今年の GDP の差が2兆円であっても、経済成長率は経済規模
によって変化する点に注意する必要があります。⑤1960 年代初
頭の日本の経済規模は、今よりずっと小さく、20兆円程度でした。
⑥この年代のある年の GDP が 20兆円で、次の年の GDP が 22
兆円だったとすると、経済成長率は2÷20＝10％になります。⑦経
済規模が大きくなった現在の日本では、高い経済成長率は見込め
ません。
⑧生産活動は資本、労働力、技術の3要素で決まります。⑨こ
の3つの要素が持つ潜在能力を最大限に発揮するとき、経済成
長率はさらに高くなると考えられます。⑩この潜在能力を最大限
に発揮したときの成長率を**潜在成長率**といいます。

11. Inflation

①Inflation is an economic phenomenon where the price of
インフレーション　　　　　　　現象　　　　　　　価格
goods continues to rise. ②A slow increase in prices boosts
商品　　〜を続ける　　　　　　ゆるやかな　　　　　　　　促進する
economic growth. ③Let us suppose that the interest rate on
成長　　　　〜と仮定すると　　　　預金金利
savings is 2.5% and the inflation rate is 5% during a period of
inflation. ④If you buy something for one million yen under
　　　　　　　　　　　　　　　　　100万円
this condition, the value will increase to one million and 50
　　　　　　　　額面　　　　　　　　　　105万円
thousand yen one year later and you will gain 50 thousand
　　　　　　　　1年後に　　　　　　　　得る
yen in assets. ⑤Meanwhile, if you save one million yen in
資産として　　　その一方で
a bank for a year, you will only earn 25,000 yen in interest.
　　　　　　　　　　　　　　　　　　　　　　　　利子として
⑥Consequently, the economy is stimulated under inflation
その結果として　　　　　　　　　　刺激を受ける(→活性化する)
because you gain more profit by purchasing things than
　　　　　　　　　　利益　　　購入すること
saving money in a bank.

⑦There are two major causes of inflation. ⑧The first occurs
　　　　　　　　　　原因　　　　　　　　　　　起きる
when the government issues more money than the people
　　　　　　　　　　発行する
need. ⑨When a large amount of money is circulating,
必要とする　　大量の　　　　　　　　　　流通する
households and companies have more money, which
家計　　　　　企業　　　　　　　　　　(前文を受けて)そのことが
increases their spending power. ⑩If the supply is not
　　　　　購買力　　　　　　　　供給

enough to meet the increased demand, the price of goods
　　　　見合う
rises. ⑪This type of inflation is called demand-pull inflation.
　　　　　　　　　　　　　　　　ディマンド・プル・インフレーション
⑫The second is that a rise in cost of materials, such as
　　　　　　　　　　　　　　　　　　　原材料
iron-ore and crude oil, could raise the goods prices and cause
鉄鉱石　　　　原油　　　　　　　　　　　　　　　　　原因になる
inflation. ⑬The inflation caused in this way is called
　　　　　　　　　　　　　　　このようにして
cost-push inflation.
コスト・プッシュ・インフレーション

11. インフレーション

①モノの価格が持続的に上がり続ける経済現象が**インフレーション
（インフレ）**です。②ゆるやかな物価上昇は、経済成長を促します。③イ
ンフレ下で、預金金利が2.5％、物価上昇率が5％だとします。④こ
の条件下で100万円のモノを買うと、1年後には105万円になり、5
万円資産が増えます。⑤一方、100万円を1年間、銀行に預金して得
られる利子は、2万5,000円にすぎません。⑥このように、インフレ
になると、銀行に預金するよりもモノを買うほうが得になることが多
いので、消費が盛んになり、経済活動が活発化します。
⑦インフレの主要な原因は2つあります。⑧第1は、人々が必要と
している以上のお金を政府が発行することで起こります。⑨多くの
お金が流通すると、家計や企業がお金を持ち、購買力を増します。
⑩需要が増えたときに供給が増えないと、モノの価格が上昇します。
⑪こうして発生するのが、「**ディマンド・プル・インフレ**」です。⑫第
2に、鉄鉱石や石油といった原材料の値上がりなど、供給者側の事
情によってモノが値上がりするとインフレになります。⑬このよう
にして引き起こされるのが「**コスト・プッシュ・インフレ**」です。

12. Deflation

①Deflation is an economic phenomenon where commodity
デフレーション　　　　　　　　　　　現象　　　　　　物価
prices continuously fall. ②Prices fall if there is a surplus of
持続的に　　下がる　　　　　　　　　　　余剰分
goods with few buyers. ③Deflation also occurs when
モノ　　　少ししかいない　　　　　　　　生じる
there is a shortage of money circulating in the economy.
　　　　　〜の不足　　　　　流通

④Japan has been in a state of deflation since 1995.
　　　　　　　　　　〜の状態

⑤During a period of deflation, companies and stores
　　　〜の期間
reduce expenses and salaries to lower prices to remain
減らす　経費　　　給料　　　低くする　　　　　保つ
competitive. ⑥If salaries are reduced, people spend less
競争力　　　　　　　　　　　　　　　　　　少ししかお金を使わない
money.

⑦That is not all. ⑧If the deflation continues, things are
　　　　　　　　　　　　　　続く
cheaper in the subsequent year than in the present year.
次の年　　　　　　　　　　　　　　　今年
⑨In other words, it means that your money is increasing in
言い換えれば
value. ⑩Therefore people spend less money because the
価値　　したがって
value of the money is increasing as much as by
　　　　　　　　　　　　　　　〜だけで
keeping it under a mattress.
お金をマットレスの下に隠しておく(→タンス貯金をする)
⑪A negative spiral, where deflation decreases the circulation
マイナスの循環(→悪循環)　　　　　　　　　流通量
of money and the resulting shortage of money in circulation
その結果　　　不足

makes the deflation worse, is called a "deflationary

spiral".

デフレ・スパイラル

12. デフレーション

①持続的にモノの価格が下がる経済現象が**デフレーション（デフレ）**です。②モノが十分にあるのに、それを買いたい人が少ないと、価格は下がります。③また、貨幣の流通量が少ないと、デフレが発生します。

④日本経済は、1995 年頃からデフレ状態にあります。⑤デフレ下では、企業や商店は安さを競うことになり、従業員の給料を下げたり、経費を削減したりして価格を下げます。⑥給料が下がれば、人々が使うお金も減ります。

⑦それだけではありません。⑧デフレが続くということは、今年よりも来年のほうがモノを安く買えることになります。⑨見方を変えれば、お金の価値が上がっていることになります。⑩お金をタンスにしまっておくだけで財産が増えるのですから、人々はますますお金を使わなくなります。

⑪このように、デフレがさらに貨幣の流通量を減らしてデフレを深刻化させるという悪循環に陥る状態が「**デフレ・スパイラル**」です。

13. Economic Indicators and Indexes

①The government and the Bank of Japan (BOJ) (see p.98)
日本銀行

publish documents to be used in analyzing and forecasting
発表する 資料　　　　　　　　　分析　　　　　予測

the economy.

②The Cabinet Office gathers statistical results and publishes
内閣府　　　　　　集計する　統計結果　　　　　　発表する

them as the "Index of Business Conditions" (see p.36) every
景気動向指数

month. ③The Cabinet Office also publishes monthly reports
公開する

such as the "Monthly Economic Report", the "Economic
月例経済報告レポート　　　　　　　景気ウォッチャー調査

Watchers Survey", and the "Consumer Confidence Survey".
消費動向調査

④Additionally, it issues the "White Paper on the Economy
さらに　　　　　　公表する　経済財政白書

and Public Finance" once a year.

⑤Meanwhile, the BOJ gathers and compiles surveys and
一方　　　　　　　　　　　　　集計する　　調査

publishes the "Tankan" (see p.38) quarterly. ⑥The BOJ
日銀短観　　　　　　年に4回

publishes the "Monthly Report of Recent Economic and
金融経済月報

Financial Developments", which is the economic status
状況

concluded from their monthly meeting, as well as
～で判断された　　　　　　　　　　　　　それと同様に～

publishing the biannual "Outlook for Economic Activity and
年に2回の　経済・物価情勢の展望

Prices" in which economic forecasts are compiled.

⑦Incidentally, the "corporate goods price index (CGPI)",
また(ついでながら)　　企業物価指数

which is issued monthly by the BOJ serves as an important
発行する　　　　　　　　　　　　　　　～として役立つ

reference along with the "consumer price index", which is
参考資料　　～とともに　　消費者物価指数

published monthly by the Ministry of Internal Affairs and
総務省

Communications (MIC) (see p.40).

13. 景気をみる指標

①景気の推移を分析・予測するために、政府と日本銀行 (p.98
参照) では、さまざまな統計やアンケートをとり、これらを公開
しています。

②内閣府は、毎月の統計結果を集計し、「**景気動向指数** (p.36 参
照)」として発表しています。③また、「**月例経済報告レポート**」や、
「**景気ウォッチャー調査**」、「**消費動向調査**」の結果を、毎月レポ
ートとして公開しています。④さらに、年に 1 度「**経済財政白書**」
を公表しています。

⑤一方、日本銀行は、アンケート調査の結果を集計してまとめた
「**日銀短観** (p.38 参照)」を年に 4 回発表しています。⑥日銀が
発表するレポートとしては、金融政策決定会合で決めた景気判断
をまとめた「**金融経済月報**」を毎月発行するほか、経済の見通し
をまとめた「**経済・物価情勢の展望**」を年に 2 回発表しています。

⑦また、日銀が毎月発表する**企業物価指数**は、総務省が発表する
消費者物価指数とならんで、景気動向を予測するための重要な指
数として参考にされています (p.40 参照)。

14. Index of Business Conditions

①The "Index of Business Conditions", issued monthly by the
景気動向指数　　　　　　　　　　　　　公表された
Cabinet Office, is an indicator of the short-term
内閣府　　　　　　　　経済指標　　　　　　短期的な
performance of the economy. ②There are 2 types of
動き
processes to calculate an index of business conditions: the
過程　　　算出する
composite index (CI) and the diffusion index (DI).
各種の要素から成る　　　　　　　拡散
③This index is processed with 28 basic indicators.
　　　　　　～から加工される(→算出される)
④There are basic indexes which are categorized in three
　　　　　　　　　　　　　　　　　　～に分類される
ways: eleven leading indexes which reflect the prospective
　　　　　先行指数　　　　　　　　　反映する　　予想された
movement of the economy, eleven coincident indexes which
　　　　　　　　　　　　　　　　　　一致指数
reflect the current status of the economy and six lagging
　　　　現在の　　　　　　　　　　　　　　　　　遅行指数
indexes which reflect the movement of the economy
belatedly.
遅れて
⑤The CI is calculated by combining the movements of
　　　　　　　　　　　　合成して
basic indexes which indicates the scale of the economy.
　　　　　　　　　　示す　　大きさ
⑥On the other hand, the DI is calculated by adding the
一方　　　　　　　　　　　　　　　　　　加算して
points of indexes which is 1 if the value is higher compared
　　　　　　　　　　　　　　　　　　　　　　　　　　～と比べて
to the previous research, or -1 if the value has lowered.
　　　　以前の

⑦The DI reveals the rise and fall of the economy.
　　　　　　明らかにする

⑧Although, the CI is released as the "Index of Business
　〜ではあるが　　　　　　　公表される
Conditions", the DI is also attached for reference
　　　　　　　　　　　　　　　〜も添えられる　　　　　参考のために
purposes.

14. 景気動向指数

①「**景気動向指数**」は、内閣府が毎月発表している、短期的な景気の動きを示す指数です。②景気動向指数には、CI（コンポジット・インデックス）と DI（ディフュージョン・インデックス）の２つの算定方法があります。

③この指数は 28 項目の基礎指数から算出します。④基礎指数は、景気変動を数カ月早めに反映する 11 種類の**先行指数**、景気変動と一致して動く 11 種類の**一致指数**、景気の変動に遅れて反応する６種類の**遅行指数**の３つに分かれています。

⑤構成する指数の動きを合成して算出する CI は、景気変動の大きさを反映します。

⑥一方 DI は、指数が前回の調査に比べてよい方向にむかっていれば＋１ポイント、悪い方向にむかっていれば－１ポイントとし、これを加算して算出します。⑦DI は、景気が上がっているか下がっているかの傾向を示します。

⑧景気動向指数は CI で公表されるようになりましたが、DI も参考として公表されています。

15. Tankan

①The Bank of Japan conducts quarterly surveys and
日本銀行 行う 4半期調査
publishes the compiled results in the "Tankan". ②The
発表する まとめられた結果 ～として 日銀短観
official name of the survey is "Short-Term Economic Survey
正式名 全国企業短期経済観測調査
of Enterprises in Japan". ③However, the document compiled
書類
from it is known as the "Tankan" even in foreign countries.

④The Tankan is one of the most representative indicators of
代表的な 指標
the Japanese economy and is used as a reference worldwide
参考 世界的な
by anyone involved in the market, which influences the
～に関わった 影響を与える
movement of stock prices and the exchange rate.
動き 株価 為替レート
⑤The participants of the survey are 10 thousand companies
参加者 会社
selected from about 210 thousand companies with market
～から選ばれた 資本金
capitalization of more than 20 million yen with the
～以上の 2,000万円 ～を除いた
exception of financial institutions. ⑥There are two types of
金融機関
questions, of which one is multiple choice, with answer
そのうちの～ 多項選択
choices of "good", "not so good" and "bad", and the other
involves questions requiring number answers, regarding
～を含む ～を必要とする
debts, assets, sales and employment costs. ⑦The answers are

organized by the size and category of the companies and then
整理される　　　　　　種類

aggregated. ⑧Since this indicator is calculated in the same
集計される

way as the DI (see p.36), it is suitable for predicting the
適している　　　予測

direction the economy will take.
方向

15. 日銀短観

①日本銀行は、4半期ごとに企業にアンケート調査を行ない、その結果をまとめて「**日銀短観**」として発表しています。②正式名称は「**全国企業短期経済観測調査**」です。③ただし、海外でも「タンカン」として知られています。④これは日本の代表的な経済指標の1つであり、世界の市場関係者が参考にしているため、株価や為替レートの変動にも影響を及ぼします。

⑤アンケートの対象となる企業は、金融機関を除いた資本金2,000万円以上の全国の民間企業約21万社から選ばれた約1万社です。⑥調査内容は、収益など業況や資金繰りなどについての判断を「よい、さほどよくない、悪い」の3つから選ぶものと、負債、資産、売上高、人件費などについて、数字を記入するものがあります。⑦得られた回答は、企業の規模と業種別に整理して集計されます。⑧データが**DI** (p.36参照) で加工されているため、景気変動の方向性を見極めるのに適しています。

16. Price Index

①A price index is a statistic which shows the fluctuation of
　　　　物価指数　　　　　　　　統計値　　　　　　　　　　　　変動
prices. ②It is also regarded as an important indicator which
　　　　　　　　　　　　　～と見なされる　　　　　　　　指標
is used for a guide in the financial policy of the government
　　　　　　　　目安　　　　　　財政政策
(see p.56) and the monetary policy of the central bank (BOJ)
　　　　　　　　　金融政策　　　　　　　　　中央銀行
(see p.100). ③The major price indexes are the GDP deflator,
　　　　　　　　　　　　主な　　　　　　　　　　　GDPデフレーター
the consumer price index (CPI) and the corporate goods
　　消費者物価指数　　　　　　　　　　　　　　企業物価指数
price index (CGPI).

④The GDP deflator is calculated by dividing normal GDP by
　　　　　　　　　　　　　　　　　　　　　　　　名目GDP
real GDP. ⑤It is an index which can be used to predict price
実質GDP　　　　　　　　　　　　　　　　　　　　　　　予測する
behavior the most easily and comprehensively among the three
動き　　　　　　　　　　　　　　総合的に
indexes. ⑥The GDP deflator is different from the other two

indexes in that it is not influenced by fluctuations of import prices.
　　　　　　　　　　　　影響を受ける　　　　　　　　　　　輸入の
⑦The CPI is derived from the retail prices of 600
　　　　　　～から導かれる　　　小売価格
goods or services. ⑧This index indicates the level of prices
商品　　　　　　　　　　　　　　　示す　　　　水準
that average households spend on goods and services. ⑨The
　　　平均的な　家庭　　　費やす
CPI is announced monthly by the Ministry of Internal
　　発表される　　　　　　　　　　　総務省
Affairs and Communications (MIC).

⑩The CGPI is published monthly by the BOJ and was
previously known as the Index of Wholesale Prices.
以前は　　　　　　　　　　　　　卸売物価指数
⑪This index indicates the price levels of corporate
企業の
transactions. ⑫Domestic corporate goods price index, import
商取引　　　　　国内の
price index and export price index are derived from the
manufacturer prices of 1,286 goods and services.
生産者価格

16. 物価指数

①**物価指数**は、物価の変動を知るための統計数字です。②政府の財政政策（p.56 参照）や、中央銀行（日銀）の金融政策（p.100 参照）を作成する目安になるため重要視されています。③**GDP デフレーター、消費者物価指数、企業物価指数**が主な物価指数です。④「GDP デフレーター」は、**名目 GDP**[※1] を**実質 GDP**[※2] で割って算出します。⑤３つのなかで、もっとも総合的な物価動向をつかみやすい指数です。⑥GDP デフレーターは、輸入原料の価格変動による影響を受けない点が他の２つと異なります。

⑦「消費者物価指数」は、約 600 品目のモノ・サービスの小売価格の変動から算出した値です。⑧この値は平均的な世帯が購入する家計にかかるモノ・サービスの価格の水準を示します。⑨消費者物価指数は、総務省が毎月発表しています。

⑩「企業物価指数」は、日銀が毎月発表しており、以前は**卸売物価指数**と呼ばれていました。⑪この値は企業間取引における価格水準を示します。⑫1,286 品目のモノ・サービスの生産者価格から、国内企業物価指、輸出・輸入物価指数がそれぞれ算出されます。

[※1] 名目 GDP：物価の変動を考慮しないで求めた GDP。
[※2] 実質 GDP：物価の変動を考慮して計算した数値（名目 GDP ÷ 物価指数）。

17. Overall Unemployment Rate

①"Unemployment" is a situation where a person has the
失業   状態   (= in which)

intent to work but cannot find a job. ②The "completely
意思   完全失業者

unemployed" is an unemployed person who would be able to

work as long as he/she has a job. ③It defines only a person
      ～さえすれば   定義される

who is willing to work. ④People, who do not have the
    進んで～する

intent to work, such as "Not in Education, Employment or
                            教育・労働・職業訓練のいずれにも参加していない人(ニート)

Training" (NEET), are not "unemployed" but are
                        ～ではなく―である

counted as "non-labor force".
              非労働力人口

⑤The "labor force population" is the population of people
    労働力人口

aged over 15 who have the intention of working and are able
                            意思

to work. ⑥The "labor force employed" are the practically
          就業者   実際には

employed persons among them. ⑦The "labor force

population" is the total of the "unemployed" and the "labor

force employed". ⑧The rate of overall unemployment is
                    完全失業率

calculated as the number of unemployed people divided by the
算出される   割って

labor force population, multiplied by 100. ⑨In Japan, the
                        かけて

Ministry of Internal Affairs and Communications (MIC)
総務省

researches and announces the unemployment rate every
調査する　　　　　発表する
month. ⑩This is one of the major economic indicators.
　　　　　　　　　　　　　　主要な　景気指標

⑪However, if a person works even 1 hour during the final
　　ただし　　　　　　　　　　　　　　　　　　　　最後の週
week of the month preceding the research, he/she is not
　　　　　　　　　～に先立つ
counted as unemployed. ⑫Consequently, the actual
　　　　　　　　　　　　　　　したがって　　　　　実際の
unemployment rate is thought to be higher.

17. 完全失業率

①働きたくても仕事がない状態を**失業**といいます。②失業中であり、仕事がありさえすればすぐに働ける人を「**完全失業者**」といいます。③失業者は、働く意思がある人のみを指します。④ニートのように仕事する意思がない人たちは、失業者ではなく「**非労働力人口**」としてカウントされます。

⑤15歳以上で働く意思があり、実際に働くことが可能な人口を「**労働力人口**」といいます。⑥そのなかで、実際に職についている人を「**就業者**」といいます。⑦労働力人口は、就業者と完全失業者の合計です。⑧**完全失業率**は、失業者数を労働力人口で割り、100をかけて算出します。⑨日本では総務省が毎月、完全失業率を調査・発表しています。⑩これは主要な景気指標の一つとなっています。

⑪ただし、求職している人が調査日前月末の1週間に1時間でも働いた場合は「就業者」になり、完全失業者にはカウントされません。⑫そのため、実際の失業率は、完全失業率よりもさらに高いと考えられます。

経済の３つの主体
Three Economic Units

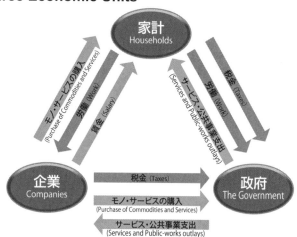

需要と供給の均衡点
The Point Where Supply and Demand are Balanced

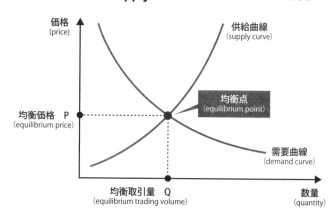

インフレーション
Inflation

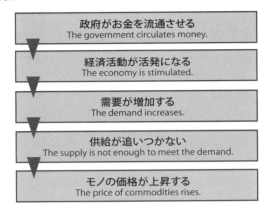

政府がお金を流通させる
The government circulates money.

経済活動が活発になる
The economy is stimulated.

需要が増加する
The demand increases.

供給が追いつかない
The supply is not enough to meet the demand.

モノの価格が上昇する
The price of commodities rises.

デフレーション
Deflation

お金の流通が減少する
There is a shortage of money circulating.

人々がお金を使わなくなる
People spend less money.

需要が減少する
The demand decreases.

モノの価格を下げる
The companies lower the price of commodities.

企業の売上げが減少し、出費を控える
The companies lose sales and reduce spending.

モノの価格がさらに下がる
The price of commodities decreases even further.

Adam Smith

アダム・スミス (1723-1790)

①Adam Smith is Scottish, regarded as the father of economics. ②He taught logic and ethics at the University of Glasgow.

③In England, as the industrial revolution started, factories were mainly constructed in urban areas, and people were gathered from farming villages to work there. ④The products manufactured in the factories were exported to the British colonies.

⑤Since the middle of the 17th century, England had engaged in a triangular trade. ⑥British merchants bought slaves in West Africa, then traded them for sugar, tobacco or cotton in the West Indies, or North America, and finally, sold these commodities in Europe. ⑦England gained enormous profit from this business. ⑧This style of business was based on the mercantilism doctrine where they gained profit from the exportation without the importation. ⑨Under the mercantilism doctrine, which was endorsed by the government, the rich and those in power profited by the sacrifice of the poor. ⑩Adam Smith wrote "Wealth of Nations" and criticized this doctrine. ⑪In his essay, he proposed that the government should maintain a society where the competition between the classes was liberalized. ⑫Even today, "Wealth of Nations", in which many basic theories of capitalism are described, is read by many people in the world.

①スコットランド人の学者アダム・スミス（1723 ～ 1790）は経済学の祖といわれています。②彼はグラスゴー大学で論理学や道徳哲学を教えていました。

③イギリスは産業革命が始まったばかりで、工場ができ、農村から都市部に人口が集まってきていました。④工場で作られた製品は、イギリスの植民地に輸出されました。

⑤17 世紀半ばから、イギリスは三角貿易を 行なっていました。⑥イギリスの商人は、西アフリカから労働力として奴隷を買い、西インドや北アメリカで、砂糖、タバコ、綿花などの農産物と彼らを交換し、その品々をヨーロッパ諸国に売っていました。⑦この取引で、イギリスは莫大な利益を得ていました。⑧このやり方は、輸入をせずに輸出だけで多くの富を得るという、重商主義にもとづいています。⑨政府によって奨励された重商主義は、消費者が犠牲になり、富者や権力者が富を得るしくみでした。⑩スミスは『国富論』を書いて、これを批判しました。⑪そのなかでアダム・スミスは、すべての国民が繁栄するには、階級を超えた自由競争が放任される社会を維持しなければいけないとしています。⑫多くの資本主義経済に関する基本的な理論が書かれている『国富論』は、現代でも多くの人に読まれています。

Chapter 2

Government
and
Economy

第2章

政府と経済

18. The Role of Government

①Government finances is the economic activity carried out
　　　　　財政　　　　　　　　　　　　　　　　　　活動　　　　行なわれる
by the government. ②Government includes the Cabinet and
　　　　　　　　　　　　　　　　　含む　　　　内閣
ministries and agencies supporting the Cabinet, as well as
省庁　　　　　　　　　　　　　　　　　　　　　　　　　　〜も同様に
local government. ③Government finances has three
地方公共団体
functions.
機能

④The first function is to prepare the facilities, or
　　　　　　　　　　　　　　整備する　　設備
infrastructure such as roads, bridges, airports, water and
インフラ
sewage systems, schools and parks, and to develop public
下水道　　　　　　　　　　　　　　　　　　　　　　発展させる
services such as medical care, police and fire departments.
公共サービス　　　医療

⑤The second function is the redistribution of income which
　　　　　　　　　　　　　　　　再配分
adjusts the disparity of income. ⑥For this purpose, the
是正する　不平等　　　　　　　　　　　　そのために
government established a progressive taxation system
　　　　　　確立した　　　累進課税制度
where more tax is collected from the rich than the poor.
　　…より多くの税金

⑦This function also includes the Social Security System,
　　　　　　　　　　　　　　　　社会保障制度
such as Public Assistance to financially assist the poor,
　　　　公的扶助　　　　　　　　　　援助する　貧しい人
Social Insurance such as Unemployment Insurance and
社会保険　　　　　　　　雇用保険
Pension Insurance, Social Welfare such as welfare for the
年金保険　　　　　社会福祉　　　　　　　　老人福祉

elderly and the disabled and public health for epidemic
　　　　　　障がい者　　　　　　公衆衛生　　　　　　　伝染病予防
prevention and maintenance of water and sewage systems.
　　　　　　　　　　　管理
⑧The third function is to stabilize the economy by financing
　　　　　　　　　　　　　　　　安定させる　　　　　　　　　助成する
public works and adjusting taxes as the economy changes.
公共事業　　　　　　　調整する

18. 政府の役割

①**政府**の行なう経済活動を**財政**といいます。②政府とは**内閣**とその下にある省庁のことをいい、**地方公共団体**も政府に含まれます。③財政には大きく３つの機能があります。

④１つは、道路、橋、空港、上下水道、学校、公園などの**社会資本**と呼ばれる設備を整え、医療、警察、消防などの**公共サービスを充実させる機能**です。

⑤２つめは、所得の不平等を是正するために**所得の再分配をする機能**です。⑥そのために、収入の多い人から多く徴収する**累進課税制度**をとっています。⑦その機能には、貧しい人の生活費を援助する「公的扶助」、雇用保険や年金保険などの「社会保険」、老人福祉や障がい者福祉などの「社会福祉」、伝染病の予防や上下水道の管理などの「公衆衛生」などの**社会保障制度**も含まれます。

⑧３つめは、景気が変動したときに、税金の増減や公共事業の実施を調節したりして**経済を安定させる機能**です。

19. The Budget of the Government

①In Japan the government fiscal year starts on April first and
会計年度

ends on March 31st. ②Income received during this period is
収入

annual revenue, and annual expenditure is the total expenses
歳入　　　　　　　　歳出　　　　　　　　　　　　　支出

paid out. ③The annual revenues and expenditures are calculated
支払われた　　　　　　　　　　　　　　　　　　　計算された

by ministries in advance, and the cabinet accordingly prepares
省庁　　　あらかじめ　　　　内閣　　　それにしたがって　作成する

a budget, which is then finalized in the Diet. ④The budget is
予算　　　　　　　　　　議決される　　国会

divided into a general and a special account budget.
分けられる　　一般の　　　特別会計予算

⑤The general account budget for the year 2019 is 101.4 trillion
兆

yen. ⑥The breakdown of revenues are as follows: tax revenues
内訳　　　　　　　　　　　　　　　以下のように　税収

which include income tax, corporation tax, and consumption
所得税　　　　法人税　　　　　　　消費税

tax, etc. 61.6%, and bond revenue 32.2%. ⑦Bond revenue is
公債

income created by issuing government bonds, which is a
創出される　発行　　国債

government debt. ⑧The breakdown of expenditures are as
借金

follows: social security cost 33.6%, public works cost 6.8%,
社会保障費　　　　　　公共事業費

education and science advancement cost 5.5%, defense cost
振興　　　　　　防衛費

5.2%, local allocation tax grants to local governments
地方交付税交付金

15.8%, national bond redemption cost 23.2%, and
国債償還費

miscellaneous 10.0%. ⑨Every year, the Japanese government
その他

issues government bonds in a greater volume than are
量

redeemed because tax revenues do not cover expenditures.
償還された

⑩In recent years, the ratio of bond income has increased due
比率

to sluggish growth in tax revenues, and social security
伸び悩み

expenses have tended to increase in expenditures.
傾向がある

19. 国の予算

①日本では、4月1日から翌年の3月31日までを国の会計年度としています。②この間の国家の収入を**歳入**、支出を**歳出**と呼びます。③歳入と歳出は、あらかじめ各省庁で計算し、内閣で予算案が作られ、国会で議決されます。④予算には、**一般会計予算**と**特別会計予算**があります。

⑤2019年度の一般会計予算額は約101.4兆円です。⑥歳入の内訳は約61.6%が所得税や法人税、消費税などの「租税・印紙収入」、約32.2%が「公債金収入」になっています。⑦公債金とは、国債や地方債などの国の借金のことです。

⑧歳出は、社会保障費が33.6%、公共事業費が6.8%、文教および科学振興費が5.5%、防衛費が5.2%、地方自治体に分配される地方交付税交付金が15.8%、国債償還費(国債の返済や利子)が23.2%、その他が10%です。⑨毎年、税収だけでは歳出をまかなえないので、返すよりも多くの**国債**を発行しています。

⑩近年、歳入では税収の伸び悩みによって公債金収入の比率が高まり、歳出では社会保障費が増大する傾向が顕著です。

20. The Special Account Budget

①The special account budget is provided for the purpose of
特別会計予算　　　　　　　　　　　提供される　　　目的

operating a specific business that has a specific income. ②The
運用する　　特定の

projects funded from this budget are 13 business categories
事業　　助成される　　　　　　　　　　　　　業種

including annual pension, labor insurance, stable foods supply
　　　　　年金　　　　　労働保険　　　　安定した食料供給

measure and energy measures, etc.
対策

③In fiscal year 2000, there were 38 businesses subject to
　2000年度　　　　　　　　　　　　　　　　　　　　対象となった

special accounts. ④In order to eliminate the complexity,
　　　　　　　　　　　　　　解消する　　　複雑さ

administrative reforms were repeatedly implemented and the
行政改革　　　　　　　　　　　　　　実施された

number of target businesses was reduced. ⑤Examples
　　　　対象の　　　　　　削減された

include the privatization of postal services, the incorporation
含まれる　民営化　　　　郵便サービス　　　法人化

of national universities, and the incorporation of the Mint and
　　　　　　　　　　　　　　　　　　　　　　造幣局や印刷局

Printing Bureaus as independent corporations.
　　　　　　　　独立法人

⑥The actual amount of the special account budget for
実質額

FY2019 was approximately 197 trillion yen, of which social
2019年度　　おおよそ　　　　　兆

security benefits such as pensions account for about 35.6%,
社会保障給付費　　　　　年金

local financial measures costs account for about 9.8%, and
地方財政対策費

government bond redemption costs account for about 44.4%.
国債償還費

⑦The surplus is carried over to the next year. ⑧One half of it will
<u>剰余金</u>　　　　　　　　　　　　　　　　　　　<u>2分の1</u>
be incorporated into the JGB Consolidation Fund※ and the rest
<u>組み込まれる</u>　　　　　　<u>国債整理基金</u>
will be carried forward and accumulated. ⑨It is also possible to
　　　　　　　　　　<u>積み立てられる</u>
transfer surplus to the general account. ⑩According to the special
　　　　　　　　　　<u>一般会計</u>　　　　　　　　<u>～によると</u>
account settlement for FY2019, the surplus after deducting annual
<u>決済</u>　　　　　　　　　　　　　　　　　<u>差し引いた</u>　<u>歳出</u>
expenditure from annual revenue was 9.3 trillion yen.
　　　　　　　<u>歳入</u>

20. 特別会計予算

①**特別会計予算**は、特定の収入がある特定の事業を運用する目的で設けられています。②特別会計予算の対象となる事業は、年金、労働保険、食料安定供給対策、エネルギー対策など、13事業です。③2000年度には、特別会計の対象事業は38ありました。④その複雑さを解消するために、繰り返し行政改革が行われ、対象事業を削減しました。⑤その例としては、郵政民営化、国立大学法人化、造幣局や印刷局の独立法人化などが挙げられます。

⑥2019年度の特別会計予算の実質額は、約197兆円で、内訳は年金などの社会保障給付費が約35.6%、地方財政対策費が約9.8%、国債償還費が約44.4%などです。

⑦剰余金は翌年度に繰り越されます。⑧その2分の1は**国債整理基金**※に組み入れられ、残りは繰り越されて積み立てられます。⑨一般会計に繰り入れることも可能です。⑩2019年度の特別会計決算によると、歳入から歳出を差し引いた剰余金は9.3兆円でした。

※ 国債の償還等を安定して行なうために設置された基金で、毎年度、国債残高の一定割合を一般財源から繰り入れて償還財源として積み立てている。

21. Government Bond

①A government bond is a national debt. ②A government bond
　国債　　　　　　　　　　　　　　　　　　借金
is issued when the tax revenues do not cover the
発行される　　　　　　　　　　　　　　　　　　　　　　負担する
expenditures. ③Local governments also issue local bonds, and
歳出　　　　　　　　地方自治体　　　　　　　　　　　地方債
together with government bonds are called public bonds. ④In
　　　　　　　　　　　　　　　　　　　　　　　　公債
2019, the monetary amount of public bonds exceeded 1,122
　　　　　合計金額　　　　　　　　　　　　　超えた
trillion yen which included national bonds in the amount of
兆　　　　　　　　　含んだ
897 trillion yen.

⑤In fact, a financial act, passed in 1947 for national finance,
　　実は　　　財政法
banned government bonds with the exception of government
禁止した　　　　　　　　　　　　　　　例外　　　　　　　建設国債
construction bonds to be used for the construction of public

facilities. ⑥However, the "Special deficit-financing bond law"
公共施設　　　　　　　　　特例公債法
was passed in 1965 and the first deficit bond was issued to
　　　　　　　　　　　　　　　　　　赤字国債
cover the revenues. ⑦Since 1975, the Japanese government has

continued to issue deficit bonds every year with the exception
　　　　　　　　　　　　　　　　　　　　　　　　　　　〜を除いて
of the 3 years from 1990 to 1993.

⑧The breakdown of Japanese government bond investors is:
　　　内訳　　　　　　　　　　　　　　　　　　　　　投資家
banking organizations (such as JP Bank) 14.4%, life and
金融機関　　　　　　　　　　　ゆうちょ銀行

non-life insurance organizations 21.1%, public pension and
生命保険会社と損害保険会社　　　　　　　　　　　　公的年金
pension funds 7.0%, Bank of Japan 47.2%, foreign investors
年金基金
7.7%, personal investors 1.3%, and others 1.0%. ⑨BOJ's JGB
　　　　　　　　　　　　　　　　　　　　　　　　　日本国債
holdings have continued to increase since the "easing of
　　　　　　　　　　　　　　　　　　　　　　　異次元緩和
another dimension" in 2013, and nearly quadrupled to about
　　　　　　　　　　　　　　　　　　　　4倍の
500 trillion yen.

21. 国債

①**国債**は、国の借金です。②国の歳出を税収だけでまかないきれないので、国が発行する債券です。③地方自治体も**地方債**を発行しており、国債とあわせて**公債**といいます。④2019 年には普通国債の残高が 897 兆円、国と地方を合わせた公債の残高は1,122 兆を超えています。

⑤実は、1947 年に国の財政に関する法律として制定された財政法では、国債の発行を禁止し、例外として公共施設を建設する費用に関してだけ**建設国債**の発行を認めています。⑥しかし、1965 年に特例公債法が制定され、初めて歳入を補てんするために**赤字国債**が発行されました。⑦その後、1975 年から赤字国債は発行され続けています（1990 ～ 1993 年を除く）。

⑧2020 年 3 月時点で、国債の保有者は、ゆうちょ銀行などの金融機関が全体の 14.4%、生損保が 21.1%、公的年金と年金基金で 7.0%、日本銀行が 47.2%、海外が 7.7%、個人投資家が 1.3%、その他が 1.0% です。⑨日銀の国債保有額は、2013 年の「異次元緩和」以来増え続け、4 倍近くの約 500 兆円に達しています。

22. Financial Policy

①The financial policy is determined by the national government
財政政策　　　　　　　　　　　決まる

who primarily implements public investment and tax planning,
　　主に　　　　実施する　　　公共投資　　　　　　租税対策

and subsidizes finances, in order to improve the economy. ②It is
　　補助金を出す　　　　　　　　　　　改善する

one of the most important economic policies of Japan along

with the monetary policies established by the Bank of Japan.
　　　　金融政策　　　　　　　　　　　　　日本銀行

③At one time, public investment was an effective aid to
　　かつて　　　　　　　　　　　　　　　効果的な助け

economic recovery. ④Once the government constructed
　　　　　回復　　　いったん～すると　　　　　建設した

infrastructure such as roads, industry improved around them,
インフラ　　　　　　　　　　産業

employment further increased, and consequently demand
雇用　　　より一層　　　　　　　　その結果　　　需要

increased. ⑤However, since some economists think that
　　　　　しかし　　　～なので

public investment has become ineffective, the budget for
　　　　　　　　　　　　効果がない　　　予算

public investment is decreasing.

⑥Tax planning is a policy under which the government
　　　　　　　　　　　　　そのもとで～

reduces taxes to stimulate the economy. ⑦If the government
減少させる　　　刺激する

adopts tax reductions, households and businesses acquire
実施する　減税　　　　家計　　　　企業　　　得る

money to spend on goods and services. ⑧Although the fiscal
　　　　　　　　商品（モノ）　　　　　　　　財源（税収）

revenue of the government is reduced, the government can

collect revenues through consumption and income taxes.
集める　　　　　　　消費税と所得税

⑨The government sometimes pays a part of the expenses
　　　　　　　　　　　　　　　　　　　　　　～の一部　費用

for developing private or municipality business in the form
促進する　　民間　　　自治体　　　事業　　　～の形で

of subsidies. ⑩Nowadays the government provides tax
補助金　　　　　　　　　　　　　　　　　　準備する

reductions^{※1} and subsidies^{※2} to encourage consumption.
　　　　　　　　　　　　　　　　　　　奨励する

22. 財政政策

①**財政政策**とは、政府が国の経済状態をよくするために、主に**公共投資**と**租税対策**を行なったり、補助金を出したりすることです。②日本銀行が行なう金融政策とともに、わが国の最も重要な経済政策です。

③かつて、公共投資をすると景気が回復する時代がありました。④道路というインフラが整備されると、周囲に産業がおこり、雇用が増えて需要が拡大しました。⑤しかし、その効果は薄れているともいわれ、公共事業費は年々減少しています。

⑥租税対策では、**減税**によって景気の回復をはかります。⑦減税をすると、家計や企業が使えるお金が増え、モノやサービスが売れます。⑧減税で政府の税収は一時的に減りますが、政府に入る消費税や所得税が増えます。

⑨また、政府は、民間や自治体の事業を促進するために、資金の一部を補助金として負担することがあります。⑩最近では、消費を促す形の減税^{※1}や補助金^{※2}が実施されています。

※1 エコカー減税やグリーン投資減税など。
※2 エコカー補助金や家電製品のエコポイントなど。

23. Primary Balance

①Japan has the largest budget deficit among the major
財政赤字   主要な

developed countries. ②The government promotes the "fiscal
先進国   進めている   財政の

consolidation policy". ③The indicator used for the target
再建→健全化   指標   目標値

value is called the "primary balance" which shows the
              基礎的財政収支

financial balance of the government. ④The primary balance

is the difference between revenues and expenditures of the
                          歳入   歳出

government, eliminating the amount of the national bonds
            ～を除いて   金額   国債

and the redemption and interest payment (see p.71). ⑤The
      償還   利払い

index shows whether the tax revenue suffices to meet the
            ～かそれとも…か   ～に十分である

required expenses to implement the policies or not. ⑥A
必要な   経費   実施する

negative primary balance means that the government has
マイナスの   ～を意味する

spent too much and has borrowed additional money.
費やした   借金をした   追加の

⑦The primary balance of the Japanese government has been

negative since the collapse of the bubble. ⑧This might be
                  バブル崩壊   かもしれない

due to the slumping economy and the reductions in income
～のため   低迷する   減少

and corporate taxes.
所得税と法人税

⑨The primary balance showed an inclining trend from 2003※
                                  上昇傾向

58

to 2007, as a result of the "fiscal consolidation policy".
　　　　　　　　　　　～の結果として

⑩Since 2008, the basic fiscal balance has deteriorated due to
　　　　　　　　　　　　　　　　　　　悪化した

the global recession. ⑪As of 2019, the deficit is 9.2 trillion
世界不況　　　　　　　　2019年の時点で　赤字

yen. ⑫The Cabinet Office was aiming to turn a profit by
　　　内閣府　　　　　　　　　　　　黒字に転じる

2025, but it is expected to be delayed further.
　　　　　　　　　　　　　　　　　　　さらに

23. 基礎的財政収支（プライマリーバランス）

①日本は世界の主要先進国のなかで、最も**財政赤字**が多い国です。②政府は、改善するために、**財政健全化政策**を進めています。③その目標値となるのが、国の収支の状況をみる、**基礎的財政収支（プライマリーバランス）**と呼ばれる指標です。④基礎的財政収支は、国債の発行や償還・利払いに関わる金額を除いた、歳入と歳出の差額です（p.71 参照）。⑤政策に必要な経費を税収でまかなうことができているかを示します。⑥基礎的財政収支がマイナスになると、お金を使いすぎて新たに借金をしたことになります。

⑦日本の基礎的財政収支は、バブル崩壊後からマイナスが続いています。⑧これは、景気の落ち込みに加え、所得税と法人税などの減税があったためと考えられます。⑨2003 ～ 2007 年度にかけては財政健全化政策の成果もあり、改善傾向にありました。⑩2008 年以降、世界同時不況の影響で基礎的財政収支は悪化しています。⑪2019 年の時点で 9.2 兆円の赤字です。⑫内閣府は2025 年までの黒字化を目指していましたが、さらに遅れる見通しです。

※ 読み方は、two thousand three

24. The Tax System

①All people are obligated to pay taxes. ②Taxes are divided
　　　　　　　～する義務がある　　　　　　　　　　　　　分けられる
into 2 categories: national tax, which is paid to the country,
　　　　　　　　　　国税
and local tax, which is paid to the local government.
　　　地方税
③Furthermore, these are divided into two categories: direct
　さらに　　　　　　　　　　　　　　　　　　　　　　　　　直接税
tax, which is paid directly by the defrayer, and indirect tax,
　　　　　　　　　　　　　　　　負担者　　　　　　　間接税
which is paid by the taxpayer instead of the defrayer.
　　　　　　　　納税者　　　　～のかわりに
④Direct taxes are principally income tax (national tax) and
　　　　　　　　　　主に　　　所得税
resident tax (local tax). ⑤Income tax is imposed on the
住民税　　　　　　　　　　　　　　　　　　課される
yearly income of an individual. ⑥In the case of company
　　　　　　　　　　個人
employees, income tax is withheld by the company which
従業員　　　　　　　　源泉徴収される
is paid directly to the tax office.
　　　　　　　　税務署
⑦Indirect tax, for example, consumption tax is paid by the
　　　　　　　　　　　　　　　消費税
shops or the companies as taxpayers. ⑧Examples of indirect

taxes are: custom imposed on imported commodities, alcohol
　　　　　　関税　課される　輸入品
tax and tobacco tax.

⑨Tax can be regarded as a membership fee for receiving
　　　　　　～と考えられる　会費
public services (see p.48). ⑩The public services, which we
公共サービス

can receive from the national government, are provided
提供される

equally to the poor, although rich people pay more tax than
低所得者

the poor as a result of a progressive taxation system.
～の結果として　　　　累進課税制度

⑪Resulting from this redistribution of income, disparity in
～によって　　　　　再分配　　　　　　　　　格差

income levels is being adjusted.
是正される

24. 税制

①すべての国民は税金を納める義務があります。②税金には国に納める**国税**と、地方自治体に納める**地方税**があります。③さらに、税の負担者が直接納める**直接税**と税の負担者と納税者が異なる**間接税**に分かれています。

④代表的な直接税は、**所得税**（国税）や**住民税**（地方税）です。⑤所得税は、個人の1年間の所得に対して課されます。⑥会社員の所得税は多くの場合、個人に代わって会社が**源泉徴収**をして納税します。

⑦間接税は、**消費税**のように店や会社などの納税義務者を通して納める税金です。⑧輸入品にかかる**関税**、**たばこ税**、**酒税**なども間接税です。

⑨税金は、国からの公共サービス（p.48参照）を受けるための会費ととらえることができます。⑩所得税には**累進課税制度**があるので、所得の多い人はより多く税金を納めますが、国から受けられる公共サービスは所得の少ない人にも平等です。⑪このような**所得の再分配**により、格差が是正されます。

25. The Increase in Consumption Tax

①In Japan, as a result of the "declining birth rate and
　　　　　　　　　　　　　　　　　　出生率の減少(→少子)
aging population", the elderly population, those older
人口の老齢化(→高齢化)　　　　高齢者
than 65 years of age, is increasing and the younger population
　　　　　　　　　　　　　増加している
is decreasing. ②In 2019, the elderly population reached
減少している
35,880,000, which represented 28.4% of the total population.
　　　　　　　　　　　　示す
③In the future, one in three people of the entire population
　　　　　　　　　3人に1人　　　　　　　　　全体の
will be elderly. ④This means that the population of the labor
　　　　　　　　　　　　　　　　　　　　　　　　　　　　労働力
force is decreasing. ⑤As the labor force decreases, the
　　　　　　　　　　　　　　　　　　　　～すると
economy stagnates and the tax revenue decreases. ⑥On the
　　　　　　　停滞する　　　　税収　　　　　　　　　　　一方で
other hand, the cost of social security, which supports the
　　　　　　　　　　　　　　　社会保障　　　　　　　　　支える
elderly, continues to increase. ⑦It is inevitable that social
　　　　　　　　　　　　　　　　　　　　避けられない
security will become a burden on the younger generations.
　　　　　　　　　　　　重荷

⑧In February 2012, a bill for the integrated reform of social
　　　　　　　　　　　　法案　　　　統合された改革→一体改革
security and tax was passed in order to secure financial
　　　　　　　　　可決した　　　　　　　　　　　確保する　財源
resources for social security expenses that continue to increase.
　　　　　　　　　　　　　　　　　費用
⑨Consumption tax has been increased to 8% from April 2014
消費税
by this law. ⑩After that, the tax increase was postponed twice,
　　　法律　　　　　　　　増税　　　　　　延期された

and in October 2019, it was raised to 10% (some of the
上げられた
reduced tax rate was 8%). ⑪The increase in consumption tax
軽減税率
is said to be used for social security costs. ⑫As measures to
～に使われる　　　　　　　　　　　　　　　　　　　　政策、対策
reduce the impact of the consumption tax hike, housing
消費税増税
measures such as extensions of mortgage deductions and
延長　　　　　　　　　住宅ローン控除
cashless point reward system were implemented.
キャッシュレスポイント還元制度　　　　実施された

25. 消費税増税

①日本では出生率の減少と、65歳以上の高齢者人口が増えて、若い世代の人口が減る**少子高齢化**が進んでいます。②2019年の65歳以上の高齢者の人口は3588万人に達し、全人口の約28.4％を占めています。③将来、国民の3人に1人が高齢者になるでしょう。④これは**労働力人口**[※]の減少を意味します。⑤労働力人口が減ると、経済に活気がなくなり、税収も減ります。⑥その一方で、高齢者の生活を支える社会保障費は上がり続けます。⑦若い世代への負担が増えていくことは避けられません。
⑧増えていく社会保障費の財源を確保するために、2012年2月に社会保障と税の一体改革のための法案が可決しました。⑨この法律によって、消費税が2014年4月より8％に増税されました。⑩その後、2度の増税先送りののち、2019年10月に10％（一部は8％の軽減税率が適応）に引上げられました。⑪消費税の増額分はすべて社会保障費に充てられるとされています。⑫消費税増税の影響を軽減するための政策として、住宅ローン控除の延長などの住宅対策やキャッシュレス・ポイント還元事業が実施されました。

※ 満15歳以上の人口のうち，労働の意思と能力をもっている人口の合計を指す。

26. Public Pensions

①The social insurance system includes public pensions,
社会保険制度　　　　　　　　　　　　～が含まれる　公的年金

employment insurance, medical insurance, nursing-care
雇用保険　　　　　　　医療保険　　　　　　介護保険

insurance, etc. ②An insured person can receive insurance
　　　　　　　　　　　　被保険者

benefits according to the extent of events or troubles. ③The
給付金　　～に応じて　　　程度

public pension is a system in which benefits are contributed to
　　　　　　　　　　　　　　　　　　恩恵　　　　与えられる

senior citizens regularly, based on premiums paid during a
高齢者　　　　　定期的に　　　　　　　保険料　　支払われた

specified period. ④In Japan, all people, between the ages of 20
特定の期間　　　　　　　　　　　　　　　　　　　20歳以上60歳未満

and 60 years old, are obligated to subscribe to a national
　　　　　　　　～する義務がある　　～に加入する　　国民年金

pension plan, which serves as a basic pension. ⑤ Company
　　　　　　　　　～になる　　　基礎的な　　　　　会社員

employees and civil servants will contribute to the employee
　　　　　　　公務員　　　　　　お金を出す　　　厚生年金

pension in addition to the basic pension. ⑥The contributions
　　　　～に加えて　　基礎年金　　　　　　　保険料

from the working generations (work force) cover the benefits for
　　　　　　　　　　　労働人口　　　負担する

the aged. ⑦A system such as this is called "intergenerational
高齢者　　　　　　　　　　　　　　　　　　世代間扶養

support". ⑧As a result of this trend of "declining birthrate and
　　　　　結果として　　　　　　少子高齢化

aging population", it is expected that two active generations will
　　　　　　　　　　～と予想される　　　　　現役世代

support one elderly person in the near future. ⑨The younger
　　　　高齢者　　　　　近い将来に

generation is worried that they may not get a pension like the
　　　　　　不安に思う

current generation, and the payment rate will decrease year
　今の　　　　　　　　　　　　納付率　　　　　　　　　　　　　　　年々
by year; the payment rate in 2011 was 58.6%, the lowest ever.

⑩Since then, the Ministry of Health, Labor and Welfare
　　　　　　　　　　　厚生労働省
has strengthened non-payment measures, and the payment
強化した　　　　　　滞納対策
rate is gradually increasing. ⑪In 2019, it improved to 69.3%,
　　　　　　　　　　　　　　　　　　　　　　　　　　改善した
but the payment rate for the younger generation remains low.
　　　　　　　　　　　　　　　　　　　　　　　　　　　　　　　　　　　　低いまま

26. 公的年金

①社会保険制度には、「**公的年金**」、「**雇用保険**」、「**医療保険**」、「**介護保険**」などがあります。②被保険者は身に降りかかった出来事やトラブルなどの程度に応じて保険金を受け取ることができます。③公的年金とは、一定の期間保険料を支払う代わりに、高齢になったときに定期的にお金をもらえるシステムです。④20歳以上60歳未満のすべての国民は、基礎年金である「**国民年金**」に加入する義務があります。⑤会社員と公務員は、基礎年金に上乗せして「**厚生年金**」に加入します※。⑥現在、年金を払っている現役世代が、高齢者の年金をまかなっています。⑦このようなしくみを「**世代間扶養**」といいます。⑧少子高齢化の結果、近い将来、現役世代2人で高齢者1人を支えるようになると予想されています。⑨若い世代には「自分は今の世代のようには年金をもらえないのでは？」という不安感があるために、納付率が年々低くなり、2011年の納付率は過去最低の58.6%でした。⑩その後、厚生労働省が滞納対策を強化し、納付率は徐々に増えています。⑪2019年は69.3%に改善しましたが、若い世代の納付率は低いままです。

※2015年10月以前は会社員は「厚生年金」、公務員は「共済年金」に加入していた。

27. Local Governments

①Public works and social security policies which are
公共事業　社会保障政策

implemented by the national government, are carried out by
行われる　行なわれている

local governments. ②Examples of prefectural governments'
都道府県の

responsibilities are operations of infrastructures such as roads,
任務　業務　インフラ

ports and airports, and so on. ③On the other hand, examples of
〜など　一方

the municipality governments' tasks are various services related
市町村の　役割　〜に関連した

to the registration of residences etc, and public welfare services.
戸籍　居住地　公共福祉サービス

④Local governments are varied in finance as well as area
多様である

size; some of them obtain a large income from taxes, and
得る　収入

others are heavily in debt. ⑤The national government grants
ひどく　借金がある　交付する

the local allocation tax and subsidies to local governments
地方交付税　補助金

so that public services may be provided equally.
〜できるように　供給される　平等に

⑥Since the beginning of the 1990s, the labor force has
労働力人口

been moving from small and medium cities in local regions
地方

to urban areas because of the reduction of public works and
都会　減少

companies withdrawing from the area. ⑦As a result, there are
撤退して

many local governments which are in financial difficulties.
財政困難に陥って

⑧When gaps between regions widen, some local governments
へだたり　　　　　地域
might not use money for needed projects, if the national
かもしれない　　　　　　　必要とする
government allocates the budget uniformly throughout the
配分する　予算　　　　均一に　　　　国全域で
nation. ⑨For this reason, some people believe in the
そういうわけで　　　　　　　　　　価値を認める
"decentralization of power", meaning that local governments
地方分権
should be independent from the national government.
〜から独立する

27. 地方公共団体

①国が決めた公共事業や社会保障政策を実際に行なうのが**地方公共団体**（地方自治体）※です。②都道府県の仕事として、道路、港湾、空港に関する事業などがあります。③一方、市区町村の仕事には、戸籍などに関する業務や福祉サービスなどがあります。④地方公共団体は、規模がさまざまで税収が多いところもあれば、負債が多いところもあります。⑤国民が受ける公共サービスの内容に差が出ないよう、国が地方交付税や補助金を交付します。

⑥1990年代初頭から、地方では公共事業が減ったり、企業が撤退したりしたために、労働力人口が都会に流出しました。⑦そうしたことで、財政が悪化している自治体がたくさんあります。⑧地域の差が拡大すると、国が一律に決めた予算配分では、自治体は地域が必要とする事業に十分にお金がかけられない、といったことが起こります。⑨そこで、自治体が国の行政から離れて地方政治を行なう「**地方分権**」を支持する人もいます。

※ 法律上の正式名称は「地方公共団体」、通称で「地方自治体」、または単に「自治体」と呼ばれる。

一般会計歳入決算
Annual Revenue of a General Account Budget

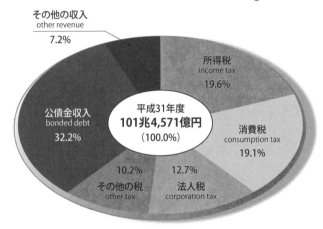

その他の収入
other revenue
7.2%

所得税
income tax
19.6%

平成31年度
101兆4,571億円
（100.0%）

公債金収入
bonded debt
32.2%

消費税
consumption tax
19.1%

10.2%
その他の税
other tax

12.7%
法人税
corporation tax

一般会計歳出決算
Annual Expenditure of a General Account Budget

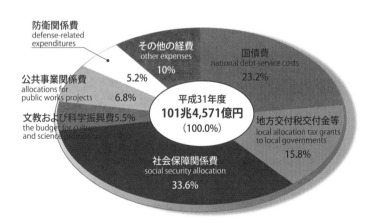

防衛関係費
defense-related
expenditures

その他の経費
other expenses
10%

国債費
national debt service costs
23.2%

公共事業関係費
allocations for
public works projects
6.8%

5.2%

平成31年度
101兆4,571億円
（100.0%）

文教および科学振興費 5.5%
the budget for culture
and science promotion

地方交付税交付金等
local allocation tax grants
to local governments
15.8%

社会保障関係費
social security allocation
33.6%

国の歳出、税収、国債発行高の推移
Transition of Annual Expenditure, Tax Revenue, and Government Bond Issuances

基礎的財政収支（プライマリーバランス）とは
What is Primary Balance?

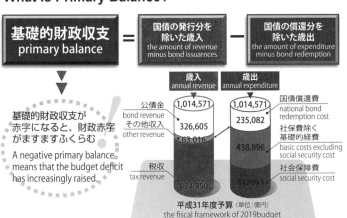

出典：財務省ウェブサイト　source : the Ministry of Finance website

Karl Heinrich Marx カール・マルクス(1818-1883)

①Karl Heinrich Marx was a German economist and a revolutionary who established Marxist economics with his friend Friedrich Engels.②Marx grew up in an affluent household with his father, a lawyer. ③He got involved in philosophy, in particular, Hegel's absolute idealism, while he was a university student, and became a newspaper editor after graduation. ④He wrote an article which criticized the German government; then married and moved to Paris. ⑤ There, he met Engels, a son of a capitalist and a scholar of social thought, who became his supporter. ⑥Eventually, he was exiled from Paris, so he traveled around, and settled in London, where the industrial revolution had already been achieved and capitalism had been established. ⑦He saw with his own eyes, the workers, in cruel situations, being forced to work hard. ⑧Marx, in his poverty, studied the economics of Adam Smith, and wrote many papers. In 1867, he had completed the first volume of "The Capital". ⑨In the book, he described the problems of capitalism as follows; "As capitalism develops, the working conditions of laborers becomes worse and they are exploited. ⑩When they become excruciating, they struggle to change society and revolt." ⑪After his death, volumes two and three of "The Capital" were completed and published by Engels. ⑫"The Capital", influenced Lenin and *Mao Tse-tung*, and inspired the establishment of the Soviet Union and the People's Republic of China.

①ドイツの経済学者で革命家でもあるマルクスは、友人エンゲルスとともにマルクス経済学を確立しました。 ②マルクスは弁護士の父を持ち、裕福な家庭に育ちました。 ③大学でヘーゲル哲学にのめり込み、卒業後は新聞の編集を任されました。 ④プロイセン政府を批判した記事を書き、その後結婚してパリに移住しました。 ⑤パリでは、資本家の息子で社会思想家のフリードリヒ・エンゲルス(1820-1895)と知り合い、援助を受けるようになります。 ⑥やがてパリから追放され、各地を転々としたマルクスは、1849 年に、産業革命が進み資本主義が発達したロンドンに落ち着きます。 ⑦ロンドンでマルクスは、過酷な労働を強いられている悲惨な労働者を多く目の当たりにしました。 ⑧マルクス自身も貧困な生活を強いられながら、アダム・スミスなどの経済学を独学し、多くの論文を執筆しました。 ⑨ 1867 年に『資本論』の第 1 巻を発表しました。 ⑩ 「資本主義が発展すると、労働者の条件は悪くなり搾取される。労働者は耐えられなくなり、社会を変えようという革命が起こる」といった資本主義の問題点が述べられています。 ⑪ 『資本論』はマルクスの死後も、エンゲルスによって引き継がれ、2 巻、3 巻が発刊されました。 ⑫ 『資本論』は、のちにレーニンや毛沢東に影響を与え、ソ連や中華人民共和国の建国につながりました。

Chapter 3

Companies and Economy

第３章

企業と経済

INTRODUCTION TO THE ECONOMY

28. A Company

①A company is an <u>entity</u> where people <u>group together</u> to
       団体   1つに集まる

earn a <u>profit</u>. ②In May 2006, Japanese business laws,
    利益

including the "<u>Commercial Code</u>" were <u>revised</u>, and a new
         商法   改正された

"<u>Companies Act</u>" was <u>implemented</u>. ③<u>According to</u> the
  会社法   施行された   ~により

new act, people could <u>establish</u> a company with simpler
            設立する

<u>procedures</u> than before. ④Since the <u>minimum</u> <u>capitalization</u>
手続き   最低限の   必要とされる資本金

<u>requirement was brought down</u> from 10,000,000 yen to 1 yen
        減らされた

and the minimum <u>board members required</u> was changed to 1
           必要な取締役

person, people could establish a company easily. ⑤<u>Following</u>
                         ~を受けて

this change, the number of companies established in a year

increased <u>significantly</u> to 76,570 in the year 2006, from
        著しく

23,228 in 2005. ⑥<u>Since then</u>, the number of newly
          以降

established companies has increased, and the number in

<u>FY2019</u> was 131,292 (see p.84).
2019年度に

⑦There are four types of companies in Japan: <u>private</u>
                           株式会社

<u>company limited by shares</u> (Ltd.), <u>general partnership</u>
                                 合名会社

<u>company</u>, <u>limited partnership company</u>, and <u>limited liability</u>
           合資会社   合同会社

company. ⑧The prominent difference between these four
　　　　　　　　目立った
types is the responsibility borne by the board members when
　　　　　　　責任　　　　　　～が負う
the company fails. ⑨A limited liability company, defined by
　　　　　　倒産する　　　　　　　　　　　　　　　　　規定された
the new Companies Act, is suited for the founder of
　　　　　　　　　　　　　　　　適合している　　　　設立者
a business venture because the founder can operate
ベンチャー企業　　　　　　　　　　　　　　　　　　　　　運営する
more flexibly than in a private company limited by shares.
　　　柔軟に

---

28. 会社

①**会社**は、営利を目的とする人たちが集まって設立する団体です。②2006 年 5 月より従来の商法とその他の法令が改正され、**新会社法**が施行されました。③この法令により、会社が以前より簡単な手続きで設立することができるようになりました。④最低 1,000 万円必要だった資本金が 1 円からとなり、取締役も最低 1 名からとなったため、個人創業が容易になりました。⑤その結果、会社の設立数は、2005 年の 2 万 3228 件から 2006 年には 7 万 6570 件に増加しました。⑥以降、設立数は増加し、2019 年度の新規設立数は 13 万 1,292 社でした（p.84 参照）。
⑦日本には、**株式会社**、**合名会社**、**合資会社**、**合同会社**と、4 つの形態があります。⑧この 4 つの会社の違いは、主に会社が事業に失敗したときの責任のとり方にあります。⑨新会社法で新たに加わった合同会社は、株式会社より柔軟に運営できるため、ベンチャー企業として会社を設立する個人創業者に向いています。

29. A Private Company Limited by Shares

①You need money to establish a new business. ②If you
　　　　　　　　　　　　　設立する
borrow it from the bank, you must pay it back with interest.
借りる　　　　　　　　　　　　　　　　　　　　　　　　　利子
③However, a private company limited by shares※ can
　　　　　　　　株式会社
collect funds by issuing shares (see p.85). ④A share is a
　　　　　資金　　発行して　　株式
unit of ownership that represents an equal proportion of a
単位　　所有者　　　　～を示す　　　　均等な　　割合
company's capital. ⑤The company does not need to pay it
back with interest. ⑥The company distributes dividends to
　　　　　　　　　　　　　　　　　　　　　分配する　　配当金
the stockholders according to the amount of shares they own.
　　　株主　　　　　　　　　　　　　　　　　　　　　　　　　　　　所有する
⑦The company does not have to do this when it is not
profitable. ⑧If the company goes bankrupt, it does not need
利益がある　　　　　　　　　　　　倒産する
to return the money.

⑨Stockholders do not have the right to directly manage the
　　　　　　　　　　　　　　　　権利　　　　直接
company unless they are concurrently a board member.
　　　　　～でない限り　　　　兼任して　　　　役員
⑩However, they can make statements about the management
　　　　　　　　　　　　　　　発言　　　　　　　経営
of the company and vote on resolutions in the shareholders
　　　　　　　　　　投票する　決議　　　　株主
meeting. ⑪If the stock※ is listed on a stock exchange,
　　　　　　　　株式　　　　　　　　　　　　証券取引所
you can trade the shares through brokerage firms. ⑫If you
　　　　　　　　　　　　　　　　証券会社

※ "share" と "stock" の違い："share" は個々の株式を、"stock" は株式一般を指すときに用
　いる。

buy the shares and you sell them when the price goes up higher, you gain a profit (capital gain) .

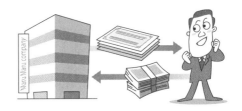

29. 株式会社

①新しい事業を始めるためには、資金が必要です。②銀行で借りると利息をつけて返さなければなりません。③**株式会社**を設立すれば、**株式**を発行することにより、多くの人から資金を集めることができます（p.85 参照）。④株式は会社の資本に対する持分を表す単位です。⑤会社側では、株式を発行して集めた資金に関して、利息をつけて返す必要はありません。⑥会社の利益が出たときに、株主が持っている株式数に応じた配当金を株主に分配します。⑦利益が出ないときには配当はありません。⑧会社の経営が破綻（倒産）したときは、会社は資金を返す必要はありません。⑨株主は役員を兼任しない限り、直接、会社経営に参加するわけではありません。⑩ただし、株主には会社の株主総会に出席して会社の経営に対して発言したり、決議に投票したりする権利があります。⑪証券取引所に上場されている会社の株式は、証券会社で売買することができます。⑫株主は、購入したときよりも株価が高くなったら、売って利益（キャピタル・ゲイン）を得ることもできます。

30. Mutual Shareholding

①"Mutual shareholding" means that allied companies,
　株式持ち合い　　　　　　　　　　　　　　　　　　連携した
including banking establishments, hold shares mutually. ②It
　　　　　金融機関　　　　　　　　　　　　　　　　相互に
has been a custom of Japanese businesses which functioned
　　　　　慣習　　　　　　　　　　　　　　　　　　機能した
effectively during the high-growth era.
効果的に　　　　　　高度経済成長時代
③The merit of mutual shareholding is as follows: it avoided
　　　　　　　　　　　　　　　　　　　　次のような　　回避した
takeovers, stabilized the management, thus stabilizing the
買収　　　　安定化させた　　　　　　　　したがって
stock prices. ④According to the Companies Act, a stockholder
株価　　　　　　〜により　　　　　　会社法
who owns more than 51% of the shares, can control the
　　所有する
company; and can even dismiss the president in a
　　　　　　　　　　　　　　解任する　　　代表取締役
shareholder meeting. ⑤To prevent the company from being
株主総会　　　　　　　　防ぐために
taken over by a third party, the company and the companies
　　　　　　　　　　　　　　（当事者の）会社　　　連携している会社
they are allied with, arrange to own the majority of the shares.
　　　　　　　　　　　　準備する　　所有する
⑥The management team can operate the company stably,
　経営陣　　　　　　　　　　　　　　　　　　　　　安定した
because the companies in the mutual shareholding are
accustomed not to interfere with each other. ⑦Additionally,
〜の習慣がある　　　干渉する　　　　　　　　　　　また
the stock price becomes steady by this because fewer shares
　　　　　　　　　安定した　　　　　　　　　　ほとんど〜ない
are traded on the stock exchange.
　　　　　　　株式取引

⑧Following the economic bubble collapse, during the
　　～の後に　　　　　　　　バブル経済
period of depressed share prices, companies lacking financial
　　　　　　　落ち込んだ　　　　　　　　　　　　　　　　　財源
resources and banks pressured by bad loans, began to sell the
　　　　　　　　　　　　　　　　不良債権
shares which they owned, and this reduced the mutual
　　　　　　　　　　　　　　　　　　　減少した
shareholding. ⑨Nowadays, many Japanese companies are
　　　　　　　　今では
operated reflecting the opinions of the stockholders.
　　　　　反映させて　　意見

30. 株式持ち合い

①**株式持ち合い**とは、金融機関を含めた親しい会社同士がお互い
の会社の株を保有し合うことです。②高度経済成長期に有効に機
能した、日本独特の慣習です。

③株式持ち合いでは、「会社が乗っ取られることの防止」、「経営
の安定」、「株価の安定」という会社側のメリットがあります。

④株式会社では、ある人が会社の株を51％保有すると、会社法
の規定により株主総会で代表取締役を解任することができるよう
になります。⑤第三者によって会社を乗っ取られるのを防ぐため
に、持ち合いで株式保有の合計が過半数になるようにします。⑥お
互いの経営には干渉しない慣例があり、経営陣は安定した経営が
できます。⑦また、株が売買される量が減るので、株価が安定し
ます。

⑧バブル崩壊後、株価低迷が続いて、財源が圧迫された会社や不
良債権を抱えた銀行が株を売るようになり、株式持ち合いは減少
しました。⑨今では、日本企業の多くは株主の声を反映させて経
営を行なっています。

31. Corporate Governance

①Corporate governance is a system by which management is
企業統治（コーポレートガバナンス）

monitored to prevent fraud. ②In the year 2007, the
監視される　　防ぐ　　不正行為

falsifications of the freshness date label by famous
偽装　　　　　　　賞味期限のラベル

confectionery makers were in the news one after another.
菓子製造　　　　　　　　　　　　　　　　　　次々と

③These affairs showed that an overreaching quest for profit
事件　　　　　　　　　　　　　行き過ぎた　　追求　　利益

is sometimes contrary to the profit of society, although it is
反する　　　　　　　　　　　　　　　　　　ではあるが

important for companies. ④Once a scandal breaks,
一度～すると　不祥事

confidence in the company is shaken and the performance of
信用　　　　　　　　　　　　　　　　　　　　　　業績

the company declines. ⑤A company is not only for the
下降する

benefit of the management team. ⑥It is for the benefit of
利益　　　　経営陣

many people such as the employees, shareholders, clients,
従業員　　　　　　株主　　　　　　取引先

creditors and consumers. ⑦These people who have a stake
債権者　　　　消費者　　　　　　　　　　　　　　　利害関係

in a company are called "stakeholders". ⑧It is important for a
利害関係者（ステークホルダー）

company to be managed in a way that fulfills the demand of
満たす　　要求

the stakeholders and bring benefits to society.

⑨Compliance means that companies conform to a rule, such
法令遵守（コンプライアンス）　　　　　　　　　　～を守る

as standards or laws of operation. The need for compliance in
基準　　　　法律　　経営

management is increasing. ⑩Shareholders are becoming

activists※ because they are troubled when the company goes
活発に主張する人（→物言う株主）

bankrupt. ⑪As for companies, the idea of corporate social
倒産する　　　　～に関しては　　　　　　　　　企業の社会的責任（CSR）

responsibility is becoming common, and that a company
　　　　　　　　　　　　　　　一般的に

must take responsibility for human rights and the
　　　　　　　　　　　　　　　人権

environment.
環境

31. 企業統治（コーポレート・ガバナンス）

①**企業統治（コーポレート・ガバナンス）**というのは、不正をしないように企業の経営を監視するしくみです。②2007年に、有名菓子メーカーによる偽装表示問題が相次ぎ話題になりました。③企業にとって利益追求は大事なことですが、度が過ぎるとこれらの不祥事に見られるように、社会の利益に反することになります。④一度不祥事が起きると、企業の信頼は大きくゆらぎ、業績が落ちてしまいます。⑤会社は、経営陣だけのものではありません。⑥従業員、株主、取引先、債権者、消費者（顧客）など、多くの人たちのものです。⑦その会社に利害関係のある人たちを**ステークホルダー**といいます。⑧ステークホルダーの要求を満たし、社会に利益をもたらす経営をすることが重要になっています。⑨また、企業が法律や基準を守って経営することを**法令遵守（コンプライアンス）**といい、この必要性も高くなっています。⑩株主も会社が倒産しては困るので、「物言う株主」になって監視するようになってきています。⑪また、企業には、人権や環境に対して社会的責任(CSR)を果たすべきという考え方も広がっています。

※ 物言う株主は、"an activist shareholder" という。

32. Corporate Bonds

①There are several methods by which a company can
<u>手段</u>

generate funds: "bank financing" and "issuing corporate
<u>集める</u>　<u>資金</u>　<u>銀行融資</u>　<u>社債の発行</u>

bonds" as well as "issuing shares". ②When a company issues
<u>株式の発行</u>

bonds, funds are collected from the public, whereas in bank
<u>一方</u>

financing, money is borrowed from a specific bank.
<u>特定の</u>

③Although both corporate bonds and stocks are financial
<u>金融商品</u>

instruments (see p.108), they differ in nature. ④When you
<u>実際は</u>

buy bonds, it is similar to a bank deposit; the principal
<u>〜と同じように</u>　<u>銀行預金</u>　<u>元本</u>

is guaranteed to be repaid with interest whether the company
<u>保証される</u>　<u>利息</u>　<u>〜か…でないかに関わらず</u>

makes a profit or not. ⑤On the other hand, stocks are not
<u>一方で</u>

guaranteed a principal, unlike bonds. ⑥Prices might fall
<u>かもしれない</u>

lower than the original price paid when profits are down. ⑦In
<u>もともとの(→買ったときの)値段</u>

contrast, the prices can rise when the company's revenue
<u>反対に</u>　<u>〜することがある</u>　<u>収入</u>

increases and you can then sell the stock at a higher price

than paid for. ⑧Sometimes you can get a dividend from the
<u>配当金</u>

company.

⑨A bond can be purchased for less than face value and can
<u>〜より少ない</u>　<u>額面価格</u>

be redeemed after a specified number of years, for the
交換される　　　　　　　ある特定の

face value of the bond. ⑩As compared to the stocks, the risk
額面価格　　　　　　　　　　　　　比べると

of company bonds is not significant but it still exists. ⑪If the
大きな

company issuing the bonds goes bankrupt, the bond would
倒産する

be repaid from the remaining resources but the amount
償還される　　　　残りの資本　　　　　　　　　総額

would be much less than the bond face value.
～よりずっと少ない

32. 社債

①会社が運転資金を集める手段として「株式の発行」のほかに、「金融機関からの融資」と「社債の発行」があります。②「金融機関からの融資」は特定の銀行からの借金ですが、「社債の発行」は広く一般から借金を募ることです。

③社債と株式はどちらも金融商品（p.108 参照）ですが、性格が違います。④社債を買った場合は、銀行に貯金するのと同じように、会社の業績に関係なく、元本と利息の回収が約束されます。⑤一方、株式は社債のように元本が保証されていません。⑥会社の業績が悪いと元本以下の価値に下がります。⑦反対に、業績が良いときには価値が上がり、高い値段で売ることができます。⑧また、配当が出ることもあります。

⑨社債は額面よりも少ない金額で購入し、ある特定の期間を経て額面の金額で償還されます。⑩社債のリスクは株式に比べると大きくはありませんが、まったくないわけではありません。⑪発行元の会社が倒産してしまうと、償還の際、社債は残った資産から支払われるので、元本割れを起こすこともあります。

33. Mergers and Acquisition (M&A)

①M&A is a way in which one company acquires another or
　　　　　　　　　　　　　　　　　　　　取得する
multiple companies combine operations. ②It is a business
複数の　　　　　　　統合する　経営　　　　　　　　　業務提携
alliance which includes business transfers, capital tie-up, etc.
　　　　　　　　含む　　　事業譲渡　　　　資本提携
③As a result of M&A, a company might expand its market
　〜の結果として　　　　　　　　　　　　　拡大する
along with sharing manufacturing hubs and dealer networks.
〜することによって　共有する　生産拠点　　　　　　販売網
④There are two types of mergers: consolidation-type mergers,
　　　　　　　　　　　　　合併　　　整理統合タイプの合併(→新設合併)
in which two companies merge into one company, and
　　　　　　　　　　　　まとめて〜になる
absorption-type mergers, in which one company absorbs the
吸収タイプの合併　　　　　　　　　　　　　　　　　吸収する
other and continues doing business while inheriting all of the
　　　〜を存続する　営業行為　　　　継承する
rights of the absorbed company (see p.84). ⑤Most mergers are
権利　　　吸収された　　　　　　　　　ほとんどの
absorption-type because procedures for consolidation-type
　　　　　　　　　　手続き
mergers are complicated. ⑥Acquisition is when an acquired
　　　複雑である　　　買収　　　　　　売り手企業
company sells its stock to the acquiring company and hands
　　　　　　　　　　買い手企業　　　　　　　　譲渡する
over the right of management. ⑦It is possible to exchange the
　　　　　　　　　　　　　　　　　　　　交換する
stock of the acquired company for those of the acquiring
　　　　　　　　　　　　　　それら(=株)
company if the acquiring company does not have funds.

⑧When an acquiring company wants to buy a large amount of
　　　　　　　　　　　　　　　　　　　大量の

stock, it advertises to the public through newspapers offering to
　　　　 公告を出す　　　　　　　　　　　　　　　　　　　　　 申し出ること
buy company stock at a higher than market price and locating
　　　　　　　　　　　　　　　　　　　　　　　　　　　　　　　 探すこと
stockholders who want to sell their stock.
⑨This process of buying stock is called a "tender offer※".
　　　　　　　　　　　　　　　　　　　　　 株式公開買い付け
⑩The number of M&A cases in Japan decreased from 2006 to
2010, but then turned to increase again.

33.M&A（企業買収・合併）

①**M&A** とは、企業が他の企業を**買収**したり、複数の企業が経営を統合（**合併**）したりすることを指します。②**事業譲渡**や**資本提携**なども含めた企業間の提携のことです。③M&A により、生産拠点や販売路を共有し、市場が拡大するという相乗効果も見込まれます。④合併には、２つ以上の企業が合体して１つの企業になる**新設合併**と、１つの企業が存続し、もう１つの企業の権利が存続企業に継承される**吸収合併**があります（p.84 参照）。⑤新設合併は新たな事務手続きが煩雑（はんざつ）なので、合併の多くが吸収合併です。⑥**買収**は、売り手企業が買い手企業に株式を売却して経営権を譲渡します。⑦買い手企業に資金がない場合、売り手と買い手の**株式交換**することで他社を買収することも可能です。
⑧買い手企業が大量の株式を買いたいときは、新聞に「普通よりも高い価格で株を買い取る」という情報を載せ、株を売りたい人を集めます。⑨こうして株を買い集める方法が**株式公開買い付け（TOB※）**です。⑩日本での M&A の件数は、2006 ～ 2010 年まで減少しましたが、その後再び増加に転じました。

※ 株式公開買い付けを米国では tender offer、イギリスでは takeover bid、日本では TOB という。

株式会社設立の推移

Transition of the Formation
of a Private Company Limited by Shares

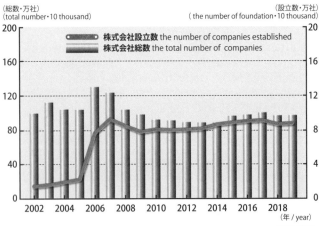

（総数・万社）
(total number・10 thousand)

（設立数・万社）
(the number of foundation・10 thousand)

出典：法務省
source ： the Ministry of Justice

M&A の手法の一部
Some Methods of M&A

- M&A
  merger and acquisition
  - 買収 acquisition
    - 株式取得 share acquisition
    - 営業譲渡 transfer of business
  - 合併 merger
    - 吸収合併 absorption-type merger
    - 新設合併 consolidation-type merger

株式のしくみ
How Shares Work

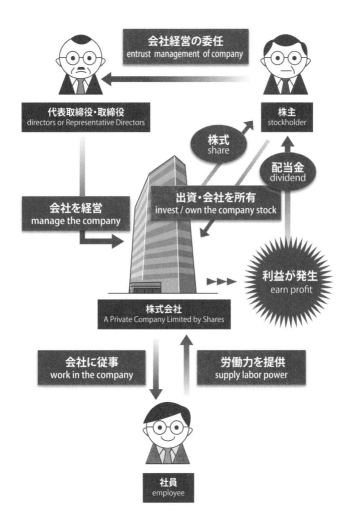

John Maynard Keynes ジョン・M・ケインズ (1883〜1946)

①British economist, John Maynard Keynes (1883~1945) is the founder of Keynes economics, on which macroeconomics is based. ②He lectured about money, credit and price at Cambridge University, and showed considerable talent at applying economic theory to practical problems as a bureaucrat, working for a time in an official government position. ③He was also known as an investor.
④The economics of that time cannot explain the high level of unemployment, 25 % using the existing theory. ⑤In that circumstance, Keynes pointed out that involuntary unemployment existed as well as voluntary unemployment, which had been caused by the pressure of labor unions. ⑥He insisted that expansion of demand decreased the involuntary unemployment which caused the shortage of effective demand. ⑦ When the world economy slid into a recession following the Great Depression of the United States, Keynes thought that it would take a long time to recover, if the government did nothing according to the classical theory. ⑧In "The General Theory of Employment, Interest and Money", which was published in 1936, he proposed a new logic to increase employment in the middle of a depression. ⑨He recommended that the government should increase public-works projects using tax money to boost the employment. ⑩In 1933, the President of the United States, Franklin Delano Roosevelt, was open to Keynes' logic and immediately implemented the New Deal program.

①イギリスの経済学者ジョン・メイナード・ケインズ（1883 〜 1946）は、マクロ経済学の原点であるケインズ経済学の創始者です。②ケインズはケンブリッジ大学で貨幣と金融を教えていたほか、官僚など実務家として手腕を発揮した時期もありました。③また、投資家としても有名でした。
④それまでの経済学の理論では、1930 年代にみられた 25% もの失業率を説明できませんでした。ケインズはそれに気づいて、新たな理論を構築しました。⑤そのなかで、ケインズは労働組合の圧力などにより生じる自発的失業のほかに、非自発的失業の存在を指摘しました。⑥有効需要の不足により発生する非自発的失業は、総需要の拡大によって解消されるというのが彼の主張です。⑦ 1929 年のアメリカの大恐慌に端を発し、世界中が大不況に陥ったときに、ケインズは、ただ従来の手法（価格メカニズムに任せておくこと）では、不況が収まるまでに長い時間がかかると考えました。⑧ 1936 年に著した『雇用・利子および貨幣の一般理論』のなかで、不況の最中に雇用を増やすための新しい理論を説きました。⑨そのなかで、政府が税金を使って公共事業を起こし、失業者に仕事をつくることを勧めたのです。⑩アメリカの大統領、フランクリン・ルーズベルトはケインズの理論をいち早くとり入れ、1933 年にニューディール政策を導入しました。

Chapter 4

Finance
and
Economy

第4章

金融と経済

34. Money

①Money is the method of exchange which is used in
交換の媒介

settlement of trading commodities and services. ②Since
売買の決済

ancient times, as division of labor has grown, a system of
分業

money was developed for exchanging things. ③Money has

three functions: medium of exchange, unit of account, and
機能する   交換手段   価値の単位

store of value. ④It has three requirements: having value for
価値の保存   要件

everyone, being divided into small units and being made of

a durable material.
耐久性がある材料

⑤Early money was made from precious metals such as gold
昔の   貴重な

and silver. ⑥In the course of time, because of the
やがて

inconvenience, gold and silver were replaced by a piece of
不便   ～に置き換えられた

paper which guaranteed redemption with gold or silver (the
兌換を保証された

gold standard system, and the silver standard system). ⑦This
金本位制   銀本位制

became paper currency. ⑧In 1885 when the Bank of Japan
紙幣   日本銀行

was established, the paper currency was silver convertible
兌換可能な

currency which could be exchanged for silver of the same face
額面

value. ⑨Currently, paper currency is inconvertible, and cannot
現在では   兌換できない

be exchanged for silver or gold. ⑩Paper currencies are used in society today because countries issuing them guarantee the
保証する
value and the people trust this.
信用する

34. お金

①**お金（通貨）**は、モノやサービスの売買取引の決済に使う交換の仲介をします。

②大昔から**分業**で生産活動が行なわれ、生産物を交換するためにお金のしくみができました。③お金の機能には「**価値の交換機能**」、「**価値の尺度機能**」、「**価値の保存機能**」の３つがあります。④お金の要件として、「万人にとって価値があること」、「小さい単位に分かれていること」、「材質が変わらないこと」の３つが挙げられます。⑤昔のお金はそれ自体に価値がある金や銀などの貴金属でできていました。⑥やがて、貴金属のお金は不便なので、かわりに金銀などの**兌換**（交換できること）の保証を記した紙を使うようになりました（**金本位制・銀本位制**）。⑦それが紙幣に発展しました。⑧1885年に日本銀行ができた当初は、日本の紙幣は兌換銀券といって、額面と同じ金額の銀貨と取り替えることができました。⑨現在のお金は、**不換紙幣**といって、金や銀とは直接交換できません。⑩紙のお金が社会で流通できるのは、発行する国が紙幣の価値を保証し、国民がそれを信用しているからです。

35. Finance

①Finance stimulates the economy by moving money
around. ②In a household, you might deposit money, which
you will not be using any time soon, in a bank. ③The bank
loans money to borrowers such as individuals or companies
who are short on money, requiring higher interest than the
finance charge which it gives for savings deposits. ④The
companies spend the money borrowed from a bank for
purposes such as business expansions. ⑤In this way, financial
institutions, such as banks and brokerage firms, are serving as a
medium to move surplus money to the entities which are
short of money.

⑥A bank finances households, when we buy a house, or
companies, when they need capital investments, with money
collected from households or companies. ⑦This indirect
trade of money between a borrower and a lender is called
"indirect finance".
⑧Meanwhile, a funding mechanism in which a company

needing money issues shares or bonds to collect money

directly from households or companies is called "direct
直接に　　　　　　　　　　　　　　　　　　　　　　直接金融
finance". ⑨Brokerage firms function as medium of direct
　　　　　　　証券会社　　　　　機能する
finance and profit through commissions they receive.
　　　　　　　　　　　　　　　手数料

35. 金融

①**金融**とは、お金を融通して経済活動を促すことです。②家計で
すぐに使う予定がないお金は、一般的に銀行に預けます。③銀行
はそのお金を、資金が足りなくて困っている企業に、借り手に払
う利子よりも高い金利で貸し出します。④企業は事業拡大などに
お金を使います。⑤このように、余っているお金を足りないとこ
ろに融通する仲立ちをしているのが、銀行や証券会社などの金融
機関です。

⑥銀行は家計や企業から集めた資金を、家を買おうとする家計や
設備投資をしようとする企業に融資しています。⑦お金の持ち主
である貸し手と借り手の間には直接の取引はなく、このしくみを
間接金融といいます。

⑧一方、資金を必要としている企業が、株式や債券を発行して家
計や他の企業から直接に資金を調達できるしくみを**直接金融**とい
います。⑨証券会社は、取引の仲介役をして手数料をとり、利益
をあげています。

36. Interest

①Interest is a charge for lending or borrowing money.
金利　　　　　使用料　　　　　貸付　　　　借入

②Interest rate is the ratio of interest to principal. ③Interest rate
利率　　　　　　　割合　　　　　　～に対する 元金

is classified into two categories by period: short-term
～に分類される　　　　　種類　　　　　期間　　短期金利

interest rate which is for loans shorter than 1 year, and
短期金利

long-term interest rate which is for loans longer than 1 year.
長期金利

④There are two methods to calculate interest: simple interest
　　　　　方法　　　計算する　　　　　単利計算

calculation and compound interest calculation. ⑤Simple
　　　　　　　　複利計算

interest calculation is calculated only using the principal.

⑥For compound interest calculation, the interest is calculated
～に関しては

by the added amount of principal and previous interest. ⑦For
　　～と…の合計　　　　　　　　前回の

example, the interest for a bank deposit and a bank
　　　　　　　　　　　　　銀行預金　　　　　　銀行の融資

loan is calculated as compound interest, whereas the interest
銀行の融資　　　　　　　　　　　　　一方

of a national bond is calculated as simple interest.
国債

⑧Interest, which stays constant until the maturity or full
　　　　　　　　一定の　　　　　満期

payment date, is called fixed interest, and interest which
全額支払(→完済)　　固定金利

varies, is called floating interest. ⑨Change in an interest rate
変化する　　　　変動金利

occurs according to the balance of supply and demand.
起こる　　～に準じて　　　均衡　　　　供給　　　　需要

92

⑩Interest rates rise when more people want to borrow money,
　　　　　　　　上がる　　　　　〜したい人が多い

and, in contrast, they fall when less people want to borrow
　　　反対に　　　　　下がる　　〜したい人が少ない

money. ⑪If interest rates fall, companies borrow money as

funds easily for business investments and this stimulates the
　　　　　　　　設備投資

economy.

36. 金利

①**金利（利子・利息）**とは、お金の貸付・借入に対して支払われる使用料のことです。②元本に対する金利の割合が利率です。③金利は期間によって、1年未満の**短期金利**と1年以上の**長期金利**の2種類に区分されます。④利子（利息）の計算方法は、**単利計算**と**複利計算**があります。⑤単利計算は元本だけに利子がつく計算方法です。⑥複利計算は、元本と前回の利子を合計した金額に対して利子がつく計算方法です。⑦たとえば、銀行預金や銀行からの借り入れの金利は複利計算、国債の金利は単利計算となっています。

⑧満期や完済まで一定のものを**固定金利**、変わるものを**変動金利**といいます。⑨金利の変動は、お金の**需要**と供給によって起こります。⑩お金を借りたい人が増えれば金利は上がり、借りたい人が少なければ下がります。⑪金利が低くなると、企業は設備投資のためにお金を借りやすくなり、これが経済を刺激します。

37. Financial Market

①The financial market developed because parties had surplus
　　　金融市場　　　　　　　　　　　　　　　グループ　　　　余剰資金
funds, "supply", while others needed cash, "demand". ②The
　　　供給　　　　　　　　　　　　　　　　需要
market is divided into short-term financial markets and
　　　　分かれている　　　　短期金融市場
long-term financial markets.
長期金融市場

③In short-term financial markets, assets with maturities of less
　　　　　　　　　　　　　　　　資産　　　　決済期限
than one year are traded. ④It is a market where financial
　　　　　　　　　　　　　　　　　　　　　　　　　金融機関
institutions and companies borrow or lend funds for a short

term. ⑤Moreover, the short-term financial market is divided.
　　　さらに

⑥There is an open market, where non-financial companies can
　　　　　　公開市場　　　　　　（金融機関以外の）一般企業
trade freely. ⑦The interbank market, is where only financial
　　　　　　　　　　銀行間市場
institutions can participate in the trading. ⑧Additionally there is
　　　　　　　参加する　　　　　　　　　　加えて
a call market where financial institutions can borrow and
コール市場
lend funds for short term. ⑨The most common trade in the call

market is the "overnight unsecured call money". ⑩This is a trade
　　　　　無担保コール翌日物
in which banks borrow money with no collateral and repay it
　　　　　　　　　　　　　　　　担保なしで　　　　　返済する
the next day. ⑪The interest on this trade is the "overnight call
　　　　　　　　金利　　　　　　　　　　　　　コール金利
rate".

94

⑫In a long-term market, also called a "capital market", assets
　　　　　　　　　　　　　　　　　資本市場

with maturities of more than one year are traded in order for

companies to raise working capital. ⑬A long-term market
　　　　　　　集める　運転資金

includes the securities market which is composed of stock
　　　　　　　　証券市場

markets and bond and debentures markets.
　　　　　　　　　　　公社債市場

37. 金融市場

①金融市場が生まれたのは、一方に資金が余っているグループからの供給があり、もう一方に資金を必要としているグループからの需要があったからです。②金融市場は短期金融市場と長期金融市場に分けられます。

③短期金融市場は決済期限が1年未満の金融取引が行なわれます。④金融機関や一般企業が手元にお金がないときに短期間資金を借りる市場です。⑤さらに、この短期金融市場は2つに分かれています。⑥一般企業が自由に取引に参加できるのが**公開市場**です。⑦金融機関のみが取引に参加するのが**銀行間市場**です。⑧加えて、銀行間市場の中で、銀行間の短期の貸し借りをするのが**コール市場**です。⑨コール市場での代表的な取引が「**無担保コール翌日物**」です。⑩これはお金を無担保で借り、翌日に返済する取引です。⑪この取引の金利がコール金利です。

⑫長期金融市場は**資本市場**とも呼ばれ、企業が運転資金などを調達するための市場で、満期が1年以上の金融取引を行ないます。⑬長期金融市場には、株式市場と公社債市場をあわせた**証券市場**も含まれます。

38. The Functions of Banks

①Three functions of a bank are the financial intermediary
　　　　　　　　　　　　　　金融仲介機能
function, the clearing function and the credit creating
　　　　　　　決済機能　　　　　　　　　　信用創造機能
function.

②The financial intermediary function is to mediate between
　　　　　　　　　　　　　　　　　　　　　　仲介する
depositors or lenders who have surplus funds and borrowers
預金者　　　貸し手　　　　　　　余剰金　　　　　　借り手
who are short of funds. ③Banks decrease the risk and cost
　　～が不足している　　　　　　　減らす　　　リスク　　費用
of trading by selecting the lenders and managing them. ④The
　　　　　　選ぶこと　　　　　　　　管理すること
clearing function is where payment is made by account transfer
　　　　　　　　　　　　　　　　　　　　　　　　口座振替
instead of by cash when buying or selling goods. ⑤The credit
～の代わりに
creating function is a loop where faith money is enhanced
　　　　　　　　　　　輪(→循環)　　信用貨幣　　　強化された
by borrowing and lending money repeatedly.
　　　　　　　　　　　　　　　繰り返して
⑥For example, a bank lends money to a company, the lending
　　　　　　　　　　　貸す
bank increases the nominal funds of the company which
　　　　　　　　　　名目上の
generates the credit. ⑦If the company deposits the surplus
生む　　　　　　　　　　　　　　　　　預金する
money at the bank, the credit of the bank is enhanced. ⑧This
"loop" is then repeated.

⑨In these functions, banks carry out three services: deposit
　　　　　　　　　　　　　　実施する　　　　　　　　　　預金

96

(reception), exchange (settlement), and loan (credit).
受信　　　　　為替　　　　　決済　　　　　　融資　与信

38. 銀行の役割

①銀行には**金融仲介機能**、**決済機能**、**信用創造機能**という3つの機能があります。

②金融仲介機能とは、主にお金が余っている預金者（貸し手）と、資金が足りない借り手の間を仲介する機能です。③銀行が貸出先を選び、管理することによって、取引に伴うリスクやコストを減少させます。④決済機能とは、銀行の預金口座を利用することで現金を使わずに口座振替でモノの売買や金融取引の決済ができることです。⑤信用創造機能とは、お金の貸し借りによって信用が増えていく循環のことを示します。⑥たとえば、銀行がある会社にお金を貸すと、その会社の名目上の預金残高が増え、これが信用となります。⑦この会社が余剰金を銀行に預金すると、銀行の信用が増します。⑧この循環のなかでは、そうしたことが繰り返されます。

⑨銀行では上記の機能を受け、**預金（受信）業務**、**為替（決済）業務**、**融資（与信）業務**という3つの業務を行なっています。

39. The Function of the Bank of Japan

①The Bank of Japan (BOJ) is the central bank of Japan. ②The
日本銀行（日銀）   中央銀行
central bank, which is considered the "guardian of the currency",
                                      通貨の番人
issues the country's paper currency and is in charge of
発行する   紙幣   ～を担当して
financial policy.
金融政策

③As the "bank of issue", the BOJ issues paper currency formally
     発券銀行   公式に
known as Bank of Japan notes. ④Paper currency is legal tender
         日本銀行券   法定通貨
and is approved as legal settlement money, along with
    ～として認められている   決済   ～とともに
coins issued by the government.

⑤Considered a "bank for banks", the BOJ makes trades with
 ～と考えられるので 銀行の銀行
other financial institutions. ⑥Each financial institution has a
commercial account with the BOJ. ⑦The BOJ not only settles
当座預金口座   ～だけでなく…も   決済する
payments and receipts between financial institutions through
these accounts but also buys and sells bonds. ⑧Also, the BOJ has
                        売買する 債権   また
a role as the "lender of last resort" by which it lends money to a
役割   最後の貸し手
financial institution having cash-flow problems.
                      資金繰りの問題
⑨As the "bank for the government", the national treasury
        政府の銀行   国庫金
monies, including taxes, social insurance contributions
                         社会保険   保険金

and national bond sales are deposited in the BOJ. ⑩In
addition, the BOJ is in charge of managing the national
treasury. ⑪Furthermore, it surveys the economic
　　　　　　　その上に　　　　　　　　　　　調査する
conditions and issues statistics relating to the economy.
　　　　　　　　　　　　統計資料　　　〜に関しての
⑫Another important role of the BOJ is in keeping the
exchange rate stable.
為替レート　　　安定した

---

39. 日本銀行の役割

①日本の**中央銀行**は**日本銀行（日銀）**です。②中央銀行とは、その国の紙幣を発行し、金融政策を担当する銀行で、「通貨の番人」といわれています。

③日銀は、「**発券銀行**」という機能があり、紙幣（日本銀行券）を発行しています。④紙幣は、政府が発行する硬貨とともに、法定通貨として決済の効力を認められています。

⑤日銀は、「**銀行の銀行**」として金融機関との取引をしています。⑥各金融機関は、日銀に当座預金口座を持っています。⑦各金融機関の間の決済だけでなく、債券の売買も行ないます。⑧また、資金繰りに困った金融機関に対し、日銀が資金供給する「**最後の貸し手**」という機能もあります。

⑨日銀は「**政府の銀行**」でもあり、国民から集めた税金、社会保険料、国債を発行したお金など、国のお金（国庫金）が預金されています。⑩また、国庫金の出納（すいとう）の事務も担当します。⑪そのほかにも、日銀は経済状況を調査し、統計を発表します。⑫為替レートの安定化を図るのも、日銀の大事な役割です。

40. The Monetary Policy of the Bank of Japan

①The Bank of Japan executes monetary policy independently
<small>行なう　　　　　金融政策　　　　独立して</small>
from the government. ②The BOJ, holds a monthly Monetary
<small>～を開く</small>
Policy Meeting to determine the basic course needed to
<small>金融政策決定会合　　決定する　　　基本方針</small>
adjust the interest rate in the financial market. ③When
<small>調整する　　　　　　　　　金融市場</small>
an inflationary trend begins, the BOJ establishes policy
<small>インフレ傾向　　　　　　　　　　　制定する</small>
to raise the interest. ④As a result, companies cannot borrow
<small>上げる</small>
money easily and they reduce production and business
<small>控える　　生産　　　　　設備投資</small>
investments. ⑤Households also control their borrowing so
<small>家計　　　　　　抑える　　　借り入れ</small>
that their consumption declines. ⑥Accordingly, commodity
<small>～なので　消費量　　落ち込む　　それに応じて</small>
prices stay lower and the economy becomes stable. ⑦In
<small>低い状態を維持する　　　　　　　安定する</small>
contrast, when a deflationary trend begins, the BOJ
<small>それに対して　　デフレ傾向</small>
establishes policy to reduce interest so that money flows into
<small>流れる</small>
companies and households. ⑧Consequently, production and
<small>その結果</small>
business investments increase so that commodity prices stay
higher and the economy becomes stable.
<small>高い状態を維持する</small>
⑨The main action of monetary policy is open market operation (see
<small>公開市場操作</small>
p.102). ⑩At one time, the BOJ adjusted the "official discount rate" and
<small>かつては　　　　　　　調節した　公定歩合</small>

the "reserve deposit rate" under monetary policy. ⑪However,
預金準備率　　　　　　　　　　　　　　　　　　～に従って

adjusting the official discount rate became inefficient after the
効果がない　　～の後では

interest rate liberalization of private banks. ⑫"Official discount
自由化

rate", which has not been adjusted since 1991, is now known as

"basic discount rate and basic loan rate". ⑬"Official deposit
基準割引率および基準貸付率

rate" has not been adjusted since 1991.

40. 日銀の金融政策

①日銀は、政府から独立した立場で**金融政策**を行ないます。②日
銀では、毎月**金融政策決定会合**を開いて、金融市場の金利を調節
する基本方針を決め、金融政策を実施します。③世の中がインフ
レに傾くと、日銀は金利を上げる金融政策をします。④すると、
企業がお金を借りなくなり、生産や設備投資を控えます。⑤家計
も借り入れを控え、消費も減ります。⑥物価が上がりにくくなり、
景気が落ち着きます。⑦反対にデフレに傾くと、金利を引き下げ
る金融政策をし、企業や家計にお金が回るようにします。⑧生産
や設備投資や消費が増え、物価が下がりにくくなり、景気が落ち
着きます。

⑨主な金融政策は**公開市場操作**（p.102 参照）です。⑩以前は、
金融政策として**公定歩合**※1 と**預金準備率**※2 の操作を行ないました。
⑪しかし、公定歩合の操作に関しては、民間銀行の金利自由化に
より、金融政策としての効力を失いました。⑫現在は、「公定歩合」
ではなく、「**基準割引率および基準貸付率**」と呼ばれています。⑬預
金準備率の操作も、1991 年を最後に行なわれていません。

※1 日本銀行から民間の金融機関に対して貸し出しを 行なう際に適用される基準金利。
※2 金融機関が日本銀行に準備預金として預けることを義務づけられた金額の、預
　　金などの残高に対する比率。

41. Open Market Operation

①Open market operations are actions by which the Bank of
公開市場操作   作用
Japan buys and sells bonds and bills to supply or absorb money
公債や手形   供給する 吸収する
flowing through the banks. ②Using the open market operation,
〜に流れている   〜を利用して
the BOJ influences the money supply in the short-term money
影響を与える   短期金融市場
market, where banks borrow or lend money to each other, so that

it controls the interest rate of the "overnight unsecured call
金利   無担保コール翌日物
money" in the market (see p.94). ③The interest rate, at which

companies and households borrow funds, changes according to
変動する
the interest rate of the "overnight unsecured call money".

④Consequently, the open market operation has an effect on
したがって   効果
economic activities as a whole. ⑤When the economy is strong,
全体的に
the BOJ sells marketable securities such as national bonds to
有価証券   国債
banks to absorb money from the market; which is called the

"selling operation". ⑥In contrast, when the economy is weak, the
売りオペ   反対に
BOJ buys marketable securities from banks to supply money to

the market; which is the "buying operation".
買いオペ
⑦After the "bubble economy collapse", the BOJ adopted the
バブル崩壊   実施した

"zero-interest-rate policy", which facilitated bank financing so
　ゼロ金利政策　　　　　　　　　　　　　促進した　　　　　資金調達
that corporate lending was revitalized. ⑧Subsequently, the
　　法人向けの融資　　　　　活性化した　　　続いて
BOJ adopted the "quantitative easing policy", in which it buys
　　導入した　　量的緩和政策
marketable securities from banks to increase the deposit
　　　　　　　　　　　　　　　　　　　　　　　預金残高
balance of their current accounts (see p.104). ⑨Both are
　　　　　　当座預金口座　　　　　　　　　　　　両方とも
policies of the buying operation.

41. 公開市場操作

①**公開市場操作**とは、日銀が国債などの債券や手形を金融機関との間で売買することによって、金融機関にお金を供給したり吸収したりすることです。②日銀は公開市場操作により、金融機関同士が資金を貸し借りする短期金融市場の資金の量に影響を与え、その**市場の無担保コール翌日物** (p.94 参照) の金利を誘導します。③金融機関が企業や家計に資金を貸し出す場合の金利は、無担保コール翌日物の金利につられて変動します。④そのため、公開市場操作は経済活動全体に影響を及ぼします。⑤好況のときは「**売りオペ**」といって、日銀が国債などの有価証券を銀行に売って市場からお金を吸い上げます。⑥反対に、不況のときは「**買いオペ**」といって、日銀が銀行から有価証券を買い、お金を市場に供給します。

⑦バブル崩壊後、日銀は大不況を乗り切るために、銀行の資金調達を容易にすることにより、企業への融資を活性化する「**ゼロ金利政策**」をとりました。⑧その後、銀行から有価証券を買い入れ、当座預金残高を増やす「**量的緩和政策**」を行ないました (p.104 参照)。⑨どちらも買いオペによる金融政策です。

42. From the "Zero-Interest-Rate Policy" to the "Quantitative Easing Policy"

①In February 1999, the Bank of Japan carried out [行なった] a buying operation [買いオペ] (see p.102) and drove [引き下げた] the interest rate down to […から〜まで] 0.15% from 0.25%. ②That continued until August 2000 and was called the "zero-interest-rate policy" [ゼロ金利政策].

③Subsequently [続いて], from March 2001, the BOJ performed [実施した] a "quantitative easing policy" [量的緩和政策]. ④This was an emergency measure [非常手段] in which the BOJ continued to supply a huge [大量の] amount of money to banks through the buying operation even after the interest rate fell to zero. ⑤Banks are obliged [義務づけられている] to keep money in a reserve fund [準備金], which is a certain rate [ある一定の割合] determined [決められた] by the amount of the total deposits [預金の合計額], in their current accounts [当座預金口座] in the BOJ. ⑥The purpose of this policy is to increase the deposit balance [預金残高] of the commercial accounts, as interest rates cannot be reduced below zero. ⑦Although, the BOJ expected [期待した] that the banks would lend more money to companies as they increased [〜するとき] it's reserve fund [準備金], it failed [失敗した] to get this result [成果].

⑧In 2006, <u>concluding that</u> the economy had recovered, the
　　　　　～の判断を下して
BOJ set a <u>target value</u> and returned to the normal monetary
　　　　　目標値
policy.

42. ゼロ金利政策から量的緩和政策へ

①1999年2月に、日銀は不況対策の金融政策として、買いオペ
(p.102参照)を実施して、無担保コール翌日物金利を0.25%から、
0.15%に引き下がるよう誘導しました。②これは「**ゼロ金利政策**」
と呼ばれ、2000年8月まで行なわれました。

③続いて、2001年3月から「**量的緩和政策**」を行ないました。④こ
の政策は、金利がゼロになっても、さらに買いオペをして銀行に
大量のお金を供給するという非常手段でした。⑤銀行は、預金と
して預かる金額の一定の割合を日銀の当座預金に、準備金として
置くことが義務づけられています。⑥金利をゼロ以下に下げるこ
とができないため、この政策の目標は銀行が日本銀行に預ける当
座預金の残高を上げることでした。⑦日銀は、準備金を増やすこ
とによって、銀行が企業により多くの資金を貸し出すことを期待
しましたが、大きな成果は得られませんでした。

⑧2006年に、日銀は景気が回復したと判断して、金利の日標値
を設定し、通常の金融政策に戻りました。

43. Different Dimension Easing Policy

①The turmoil following the Lehman shock in 2008 hit Japan
混乱　　　リーマン・ショック以降の

hard, and the Japanese economy slumped for several years, partly
低迷した　　　　　　　　　　　　　一部に

due to the Great East Japan Earthquake. ②To boost the
東日本大震災　　　　　　　　　　　押し上げるために

economy, in 2013 Prime Minister *Shinzo Abe* announced the
安倍晋三首相　　　　　　表明した

economic policy of "Abenomics." ③In its monetary policy, the
アベノミクス　　　　金融政策

scale of "quantitative easing" was further expanded in order to
規模　　量的緩和　　　　　　さらに　拡大した

achieve the target of a consumer price increase rate of 2% in two
達成する　目標　　消費者物価上昇率

years. ④At the same time, they implemented "qualitative easing"
同時に　　　　　　　　実施した　　　質的緩和

to expand purchases of long-term government bonds and
購入　　　長期国債

exchange-traded funds (ETFs). ⑤This quantitative and
上場投資信託

qualitative monetary easing policy is called the "different
量的・質的金融緩和政策

dimension" easing policy. ⑥As a result, the BOJ's current
異次元緩和政策　　　　　　日本銀行

account balance rose approximately to double in two years.
預金残高　　　　およそ　　　　2倍に

⑦In January 2016, the BOJ finally lowered the interest rate
下げた　金利

on money which is deposited by private banks to the BOJ,
預けられる　　民間銀行

from zero to minus, in order to further "break out of
ゼロからマイナスへ　　　　　　　　　　　　デフレ脱却

deflation". ⑧The theory is that "if a bank deposits money
理論

with the Bank of Japan, the bank will lose money, so it will lend that amount to companies and the money will appear in
<u>出回る</u>
the market." ⑨These strong monetary easing policies pushed
<u>押し上げた</u>
up stock prices and seemed to have had a certain effect on
<u>株価</u>　　　　　　　　　　　　　　　　　　　　<u>ある一定の効果</u>
economic revitalization. ⑩However, the effects of* rising
<u>経済活性化</u>　　　　　　　　　　　　　　　　　　　<u>〜としての</u>
prices and expanding consumption were extremely limited.
　　　　　　　<u>消費の拡大</u>　　　　　　　　<u>きわめて</u>

43. 異次元緩和政策

①2008年のリーマン・ショック後の混乱は日本にも大打撃を与え、東日本大震災の影響もあって、日本経済は数年間低迷しました。②景気押上げのため、2013年に、安倍晋三首相は、経済政策である「**アベノミクス**」を表明しました。③その金融政策では、消費者物価上昇率2%の目標を2年で実現するために、「**量的緩和**」の規模をさらに拡大しました。④同時に、長期国債や上場投資信託(ETF)の買入れを拡大する「**質的緩和**」を行いました。⑤この量的・質的金融緩和政策が「**異次元緩和**」です。⑥これにより日銀の当座預金残高量は2年間でおよそ2倍に拡大されました。⑦2016年1月に日銀は、「**デフレ脱却**」をさらに進めるために、民間銀行が日銀に預けるお金に対する金利を、ついにゼロからマイナスに下げました。⑧「銀行が日銀にお金を預けると目減りするので、その分を企業に貸付け、市場にお金が出回るだろう」という理屈です。⑨これらの強力な金融緩和策は株価を押上げ、経済活性化に一定の効果があったように見えました。⑩しかし、物価上昇や消費の拡大といった効果は、きわめて限定的でした。

※ この場合の of は同格を表す。つまり「A of B」で「B という A」、という意味になる。

44. Investment

①Investing is managing shares or other financial instruments for
投資　　　　　　　運用すること　株　　　　　　　　　金融商品
the purpose of increasing assets. ②Investors are categorized as
目的　　　　　　　資産　　　　投資家
follows: individual investors who buy and sell small
次のように　個人
numbers of securities for personal profit, institutional
証券　　　　　　　　　　　　　　　　組織化された投資家
investors such as companies who trade large blocks of
(→機関投資家)　　　　　　　　　　　　売買する　大口の
shares and foreign investors who trade Japanese securities
外国の
from abroad. ③Financial instruments for investments are
shares (see p.74), securities (see p.54 and p.80), investment
投資信託
trusts, foreign exchanges (FX) and real estate. ④Bank
外国為替　　　　　　　　　　　　　不動産　　　　　銀行預金
deposits are also considered commodities to be invested.
考えられる　　　　　　　投資される
⑤An investment trust is a financial instrument in which retail
投資信託　　　　　　　　金融商品　　　　　　　　一般の
investors invest and professional investors or money managers,
プロの投資家　　　　　　　運用会社
in turn, reinvest this money into a number of financial
代わりに　再投資する　　　　　　たくさんの
commodities such as shares and bonds which they have
selected. ⑥The foreign exchange investment is an investment
in which investors invest in foreign currencies and realize
外国通貨　　　　　利益を得る
profits from the fluctuation of exchange rates (see p.124) or the
変動　　　　　　　為替レート　　　　　　　　　金利

interest. ⑦The real-estate investment makes profits from real-
estate by operating apartments for the rental income or by
　　　　　　　　経営　　　　　　　　　　　賃料収入
selling real-estate. ⑧The real-estate investment trust, in which
　　　　　　　　　　不動産投資信託
brokerage firms raise funds for buying real-estate such as
証券会社　　　集める
buildings and then sharing the profits from rentals or the gain
　　　　　　　　　　分配する　　　　　　　　　賃料
from sales, is also considered real-estate investment.

44. 投資

①**投資**とは、資産を増やす目的で、株やそのほかの金融商品を
運用することです。②投資を行なう人たちには、利益を得るた
めに少数の証券を売買する個人投資家、大口の投資を行なう企
業などの機関投資家、国外から日本の証券を売買する海外投資
家がいます。③投資の対象となる金融商品は、**株式**（p.74 参照）
や**債券**（p.54、p.80 参照）、**投資信託**、**外国為替投資**、**不動産
投資**などです。④銀行などに**預金**することも投資の一つです。
⑤投資信託は、多くの一般の投資家から集めたお金をまとめて、
運用のプロが多くの株式や債券などを組み合わせて投資する金融
商品です。⑥外国為替投資は、外貨に対して投資を行ない、為替
レート（p.124 参照）の変動による利益や金利収入を得るものです。
⑦不動産投資は、アパート経営などで賃料収入を得たり、その不
動産を売却して利益を得たりします。⑧そのほかに、投資家が
出資したお金を、オフィスビルなどの不動産を購入して運用し、
賃料収入や売却益で発生する利益を分配する、不動産投資信託
（J-REIT）も不動産投資に含まれます。

45. Risks and Returns of Investment

①In investments, the higher the risk, the greater the
〔～であればあるほど…になる〕
return. ②The risk is that the profit can be uncertain.
利益   不確実な
③Some possible risks are volatility risks, liquidity risks and
考えうる   価格変動リスク   流動性リスク
inflationary risks.
インフレリスク
④In the case of a volatility risk, the shares you own might
株   所有する
decline in price if the profits of the company are down.
下落する   ～のときに
⑤A liquidity risk is the risk that you might not be able to sell
かもしれない
a financial instrument if you cannot find a buyer. ⑥An
金融商品   買い手
inflationary risk is one where the original principal's value is
元本の
reduced relative to rising commodity prices. ⑦However,
減少する   ～と関連して   物価
inflationary risk does not occur during deflationary periods
起こる
as in recent days.
最近のような
⑧Moreover, there is the risk of currency fluctuations
加えて   為替変動リスク
where the investors' principal decreases because of currency
fluctuations. ⑨The country risk is caused by the political and
カントリーリスク   ～に起因する   政治的な
economic instability in the invested country.
不安定
⑩Investments with the lowest risks and lowest returns are

deposits or bonds with guaranteed principal.
保証された

45. 投資のリスクとリターン

①投資では、収益の見返り（リターン）が大きいほど危険性（リスク）が高くなります。②リスクというのは、期待される収益が確実ではないということです。③発生しうるリスクに、「**価格変動リスク**」、「**流動性リスク**」、「**インフレリスク**」などがあります。④価格変動リスクとは、「その会社の株を買ったが、業績が悪くなって株価が下がり、損をするかもしれない」というリスクです。⑤流動性リスクとは、「買った金融商品を売ろうと思っても、買い手が見つからない」リスクです。⑥インフレリスクとは、インフレで物価が上昇し、元本が目減りしてしまうリスクです。⑦現在はずっとデフレが続いているので、この心配はあまりありません。⑧このほかにも、購入時点より「円高」になると、利息や償還金の手取り額が減る「**為替変動リスク**」があります。⑨「**カントリーリスク**」は、投資対象国の政治や経済が不安定であることから生じます。⑩ローリスク・ローリターンである投資は、元本を保証された預貯金と、額面が全額保証された債券投資です。

46. Stock Exchanges

①The stock exchange is a place to trade listed stocks and
　証券取引所　　　　　　　　　　　　　　　　　　　　上場された
bonds. ②In order for a company to list its stock, it must meet

the listing standards set by the exchange and go through a
　上場基準　　　　　　　　　　　　　　　　　　　受ける
strict screening process. ③There are 3,836 companies listed
厳しい　審査
in Japan (as of August 2020). ④The main merit of being
　　　　　　～の時点で
listed is that it is easier to raise funds from the outside and
　　　　　　　　　　　　資金を集める
the social credibility is higher.
社会的な信用度

⑤There are four stock exchanges: Tokyo, Nagoya, Sapporo

and Fukuoka. ⑥The Osaka Stock Exchange merged with the
　　　　　　　　　　　　　　　　　　　　～と合併した
Tokyo Stock Exchange in 2013 and became part of the Japan

Exchange Group. ⑦The Japan Exchange Group's market
日本取引所グループ　　　　　　　　　　　　　　時価総額
capitalization (2018) is 5.3 trillion yen, the third largest in

the world after the NY Stock Exchange in the United
　　　　　　　　　　NY証券取引所
States and NASDAQ※. ⑧The Tokyo and Nagoya stock
　　　　　　ナスダック
exchanges have a two-section system. ⑨Generally, large
　　　　　　　　　２部制　　　　　　　　　一般的に　　大企業
companies are listed in the first section and medium-sized
　　　　　　　　　　　　　　　　　　　　　　　　　中堅企業
companies are listed in the second section. ⑩Each stock

※NASDAQ は "National Association of Securities Dealers Automated Quotations" の略語。

exchange has an emerging stock market. ⑪Mothers[※],
　　　　　　　　新興株式市場　　　　　　　マザーズ
Geodesic opened by the Tokyo Stock Exchange, Centrex on
　　　　　　　　　　　　　　　　　　　セントレックス
the Nagoya Stock Exchange, etc. ⑫These are markets for

start-ups, where the criteria for listing requirements are
起業したばかりの　　　基準　　　　　　　要件
relatively loose.
比較的

46. 証券取引所

①証券取引所は上場された株式や債券の売買取引を行なう場所です。②会社が株式を上場するには、それぞれの取引所が定めた上場基準を満たし、厳しい審査に受かる必要があります。③日本で上場している会社は 3,836 社です (2020 年 8 月時点)。④上場するメリットは、外部からの資金が調達しやすくなることと、社会的な信用度が高くなることです。⑤証券取引所は東京、名古屋、札幌、福岡の 4 カ所にあります。⑥大阪証券取引所は、2013 年に東京証券取引所と合併し日本取引所グループの傘下になりました。⑦日本取引所グループの時価総額 (2018 年) は 5.3 兆円で、アメリカの NY 証券取引所、ナスダックに次ぐ世界 3 位の規模です。⑧東京、名古屋の証券取引所では、2 部制がとられています。⑨一般的に第 1 部には大企業、第 2 部には中堅企業が上場しています。⑩また、各証券取引所には、新興株式市場があります。⑪東京証券取引所が開設するマザーズ、ジャスダック、名古屋証券取引所のセントレックスなどです。⑫これらは、上場審査の基準が比較的ゆるい、新興企業のための市場です。

※ Mothers は "Market of the high-growth and emerging stocks" の略語。

47. The Credit Rating

①A credit rating is an evaluation of credit performed by private rating firms on companies or countries, which are issuing financial instruments such as bonds or shares, using alphabets and numbers. ②Investors use it as a reference in judging investment risk.

③The rating of Japanese government bonds was at the highest level in the first half of 1990, but has declined since 2000. ④American rating companies, Moody's Investors Service and Standard & Poor's and the European rating company, Fitch Ratings have assigned Japan ratings of A1, A+, and A, respectively. ⑤This is the lowest level of "investment grade" in developed countries, lower than Singapore, Taiwan, Hong Kong, and South Korea, and on par with China.

⑥In Japan, seven credit rating firms registered with the Financial Services Agency perform corporate ratings. ⑦Beyond these 7 firms, there are many companies that evaluate financial

instruments, and rank bonds and investment trusts on
　　　　　　　ランク付けする　　　　　　投資信託
their web sites. ⑧Information on the financial market has
　　　　　　　　　　　　　　　　　金融市場
become dramatically easier to get due to the widespread use
　　　　飛躍的に　　　　　　　　　　　　　広範な使用→普及
of the internet.

47. 信用格付け

①**信用格付け**とは、債券や株式などの金融商品を発行している国
や企業などについて、民間の格付け会社がその信用度や安全性に
関する評価を、アルファベットや数字でランク付けするものです。
②投資家が、投資のリスクを判断する材料として参考にします。
③日本の国債の格付けは、1990 年前半は最高レベルでしたが、
2000 年以降、下がっています。④アメリカの格付け会社のムー
ディーズ・インベスターズ・サービスとスタンダード・アンド・
プアーズ、欧州系格付け会社のフィッチ・レーティングスは、日
本の格付けをそれぞれ、A 1、A＋、Aとしました。⑤これは先
進国のなかでは最低のレベルの「投資適格程度」で、シンガポール、
台湾、香港、韓国よりも低く、中国と肩を並べています。
⑥日本国内では、金融庁に登録した 7 社の信用格付け業者が会社
の格付けを行っています。⑦会社を評価する格付け会社以外にも、
金融商品を評価する会社が多数あり、それらのウェブサイトでは
株、債券や投資信託のランキングが行なわれています。⑧インタ
ーネットの普及で、市場情報が飛躍的に入手しやすくなりました。

48. The Nikkei Stock Average and the TOPIX

①The Nikkei Stock Average and the TOPIX (Tokyo Stock
日経平均　　　　　　　　　　　　　　　　　東証株価指数　　東京証券取引所
Exchange Stock Price Index) are representative indexes which
株価　　　　指数　　　　代表する　　　　指標
show the movement of the Japanese stock market. ②The stock

price index, which measures the economy prior to changes in
測る　　　　　　　　　　　先行の
the economy, is called the leading index and is used to
先行指標
forecast the movement of the economy.
予測する
③The Nikkei Stock Average is an index derived from the
～から導き出された
prices of 225 stocks which the Nikkei Newspaper company

selected from stocks listed in the 1st section of the Tokyo
上場した　　第1部
Stock Exchange. ④Although it is called an "Average", it is

not a simple average but is calculated by a special
～によって算出される
method developed by the Dow Jones & Company, Inc, an

American publishing and financial information firm.
出版　　　　　　金融情報
⑤The TOPIX is an index which is derived from the price of all

the Japanese companies listed in the 1st section of the Tokyo

Stock Exchange. ⑥The TOPIX is calculated, using the market
時価総額
capitalization as of the base date of January 4, 1968 (about 8,602
～として　基準日

billion yen) as 100 points, and comparing the present market
　　　　　　　　　　　　　　　　　　～を…と比べる
capitalization to it. ⑧If the TOPIX of today is 800, it means that

the market capitalization is 8 times that of the base date. ⑧These

indexes fluctuate based not only the performance of the
　　　　　変動する　　　　～だけでなく…も　業績
companies but also various factors such as interest rates, exchange
　　　　　　　　　　さまざまな要因　　　　　　金利　　　　　　為替レート
rates, the policy of the government and of the central bank.

48. 日経平均と TOPIX

①日経平均と TOPIX（東証株価指数）は、日本の株式市場の動き
を示す代表的な指標です。②株価は景気に先がけて動くので、**先
行指標**といわれ、日本の景気動向を知るために使われます。
③日経平均は日本経済新聞が選んだ、東京証券取引所の第１部に
上場している主要 225 銘柄の株価の平均値です。④平均値といっ
ても単純平均ではなく、米国の通信社ダウ・ジョーンズ社の算出
方法をもとに数字を出しています。
⑤TOPIX は、東証１部に上場しているすべての日本企業を対象
とした株価指数です。⑥TOPIX は、1968 年１月４日を基準日
とし、その日の時価総額※（およそ８兆6020億円）を 100 として、
現在の時価総額がどのくらいの数字であるかを算出します。⑦現
在の指数が 800 であるとすれば、基準日と比較して株価の合計
が８倍になっているということです。⑧日経平均と TOPIX は、
各企業の業績のほか、金利や為替レートの上下、政府や日銀の政
策の発表など、さまざまな要因によって変動します。

※時価総額とは、株価の価値の合計で、現在の株価と総発行株式数をかけて算出する。

間接金融と直接金融
Indirect Finance and Direct Finance

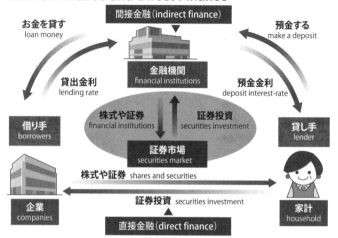

間接金融（indirect finance）

お金を貸す
loan money

預金する
make a deposit

金融機関
financial institutions

貸出金利
lending rate

預金金利
deposit interest-rate

借り手
borrowers

株式や証券
financial institutions

証券投資
securities investment

貸し手
lender

証券市場
securities market

企業
companies

株式や証券 shares and securities

証券投資 securities investment

家計
household

直接金融（direct finance）

銀行の信用創造機能
The Credit Creating Function of the Bank

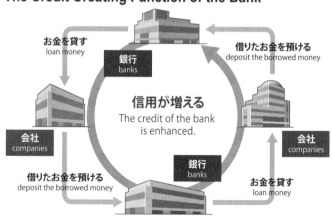

お金を貸す
loan money

借りたお金を預ける
deposit the borrowed money

銀行
banks

信用が増える
The credit of the bank
is enhanced.

会社
companies

会社
companies

銀行
banks

借りたお金を預ける
deposit the borrowed money

お金を貸す
loan money

日本銀行の３つの役割
The Three Functions of the Bank of Japan

発券銀行
bank of issue

市場
market

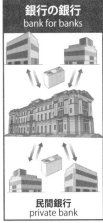

銀行の銀行
bank for banks

民間銀行
private bank

政府の銀行
bank for the government

税金
tax money

国民
the public

買いオペと売りオペ
Selling Operation and Buying Operation

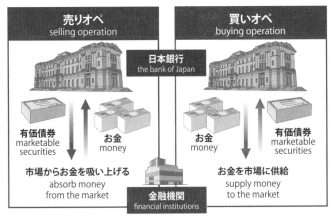

売りオペ
selling operation

買いオペ
buying operation

日本銀行
the bank of Japan

有価債券
marketable securities

お金
money

お金
money

有価債券
marketable securities

市場からお金を吸い上げる
absorb money from the market

お金を市場に供給
supply money to the market

金融機関
financial institutions

119

Liquidity Trap

流動性の罠

①"Liquidity" is an economic term which means the ease in which assets can be converted into money. ②Or the word "liquidity" indicates "money" itself.

③The condition of the Japanese economy has often been described as "an economy in a liquidity trap". ④Normally, when the interest rate falls following a quantitative ease, the availability of money to borrow increases so that consumption and business investments increase. ⑤No matter how low an interest rate is set or whatever amount of money is supplied to the market, sometimes it is not effective to stimulate the economy. ⑥That is the economy in a liquidity trap.

⑦The total deposit balance of commercial accounts in the Bank of Japan ballooned up to 35 trillion yen in 2005 from 5 trillion yen in 2003, owing to the quantitative easing policy. ⑧Consequently, business investments and consumption did not increase because banking institutes kept an enormous amount of surplus money and they did not lend funds to households and companies. ⑨Since the interest rate was 0%, companies made internal reserves and households saved money under their mattresses. ⑩As a result, money was not circulating in the economy.

⑪Keynes describe this condition in his theory of demand for money, "If the rate becomes too low, the demand for money gets stronger".

①**流動性**とは資産の換金しやすさを示す経済用語です。 ②またお金そのものを指すこともあります。

③「日本経済は**流動性の罠**にはまっている」としばしばいわれてきました。 ④通常、金融緩和によって利子が下がるとお金を借りやすくなるため、設備投資や消費が増加します。 ⑤しかし、お金をいくら市場に供給しても、景気を刺激する効果がない状態に陥ることがあります。 ⑥これが流動性の罠にとらわれた状態です。

⑦2003年に5兆円だった日銀の当座預金の残高が、「量的緩和政策」の結果、2005年8月には35兆円にまで膨れ上がりました。 ⑧そのため、金融機関などに大量のお金が余る状態になりましたが、企業や家計に貸し出されたお金は増えず、設備投資や消費は上向きになりませんでした。 ⑨金利がほぼ0%であったことから、企業は現金を内部留保し、個人はタンスに現金をしまい込みました。 ⑩その結果、世の中にお金が回らなかったのです。

⑪この現象についてケインズは、「金利が低くなりすぎると、現金に対する需要が強くなる（流動性選好説）」と述べています。

Chapter 5

World Economy

第 5 章

世界経済

49. International Currency

①International currency is currency which can be used for
　　国際通貨
the settlement of trades between one country and another.
　　決済
②The U.S. dollar, the euro, the Japanese yen, the U.K. pound

and the Chinese RMB are international currencies. ③The
　　　　　　　人民元　　　　　　　　　　　　　　　　　条件
conditions required to be considered an international
　　　　　　～に必要な　～と判断される
currency are as follows: it is internationally stable and
　　　　　　　以下のように　　　　国際的に　　　　　安定した
trusted, the country issuing it produces various goods, it can
　信用された　　　　　　　　　　　　産出する　　　　財
be traded at banks worldwide and it can be exchanged
　　　　　　　　　世界各地の　　　　　　　　　　交換される
everywhere.

④After World War II, the United States promised the central
　　第2次世界大戦　　　　　　　　　　　約束する
banks of each country gold conversion, and the US dollar
　　　　　　　　　金兌換
became the key currency (see p.143). ⑤US dollars are used
　　　　基軸通貨
for capital transactions such as international trade settlement
　　資本取引　　　　　　　　　　　　　取り引き決済
and direct investment. ⑥In addition, central banks around the
　　　　　　　　　　さらに(→また)　　　　　　　　　世界中の
world hold foreign currency reserves in US dollars. ⑦Since the
　　　　　外貨準備
1960s, when the US current account became in the red, the
　　　　　　　　　　経常収支　　　　　　赤字化する
IMF created a special withdrawal right (SDR) as a new
　　　　　　　　特別引き出し権

reserve asset that does not depend on the US dollar. ⑧IMF
（準備資産）（〜に依存する）

member countries subtract free-use currencies (US dollar,
（引き出す）

euro, yen, pound, renminbi) held by other member countries
（人民元）

in exchange for their own SDRs. ⑨In October 2016, the
（〜と引き換えに）

RMB was approved by the IMF and entered the basket of SDR
（人民元）（承認された）

currencies, increasing its international influence.
（通貨）（増加する）（影響力）

49. 国際通貨

①国際通貨とは、国と国が取引するときの決済に使うことができる通貨のことです。②国際通貨の条件として、「国際的に安定して、信用されていること」、「発行国が多様な財を産出していること」、「各国の銀行で取引が可能」、「どこでも両替が可能」といったことがあげられます。③国際通貨のなかでも、US ドルは基軸通貨といわれています。④第2次世界大戦後、アメリカは各国の中央銀行に金兌換を約束し、US ドルが基軸通貨になりました（p.143参照）。⑤US ドルは国際貿易の決済や直接投資などの資本取引に使われています。⑥また、世界各国の中央銀行では、外貨準備をUS ドルで保有しています。⑦1960 年代以降アメリカの経常収支が赤字化すると、IMF は US ドルに依存しない新たな準備資産として特別引出権（SDR※）を創設しました。⑧IMF 加盟国は、自身の保有 SDR と引換えに他の加盟国が保有する自由利用可能通貨（US ドル・ユーロ・円・ポンド・人民元）を引き出すことができます。⑨2016 年 10 月、人民元は IMF に承認されて SDR の通貨バスケット入りを果たし、国際的な影響力を高めつつあります。

※ IMF が加盟国の準備資産を補完する手段として、外貨を融資するために 1969 年に設けられた国際準備資産。

50. Exchange Rates

①The exchange rate is the ratio applied when we exchange
為替レート   比率   適用される   交換する

the currency of our own country to that of foreign countries.
通貨

②The most familiar example is the exchange of money when
     もっとも おなじみの   両替

we travel abroad. ③For example, when we travel to the
   海外旅行をする   たとえば

United States, we exchange yen to the U.S. dollar. ④This

means that we sell yen and buy U.S. dollars.
意味する

⑤The exchange rate of yen and U.S. dollar fluctuates for

example, yesterday it was 106 yen to 1 U.S. dollar although it
                                    ～だけれども

is 105 yen today. ⑥The system of fluctuating rates such as
                        変動する   ～のような

that of the yen and dollar is called the floating rate system
                            変動相場制

which is used by developed countries.
              先進国

⑦Many developing countries are using the fixed exchange
      発展途上国   固定相場制

rate system which is not influenced by the exchange rate
                              為替の変動

fluctuations. ⑧Japan also had used the fixed exchange rate of

360 yen to 1 U.S. dollar until 1971 (see p.178). ⑨China uses

the managed floating rate system at the request of developed
管理変動相場制   要求

countries such as the U.S. ⑩The Chinese yuan, which
                              人民元

currently stays at a certain rate controlled by the government,
管理されている

is in the process of shifting to the floating rate system. ⑪In
過程　　　　　　　　　　　　　　　　　　　　　　　制度

foreign exchange markets of developed countries, computers
外国為替市場

and telephones are used for trading. ⑫Exchange rates are

determined by the balance of supply and demand.
決められる　　　　　　　　　　　　供給　　　需要

50. 為替レート

①自分の国の通貨と外国の通貨を交換（売買）するときの比率を**為替レート（為替相場）**といいます。②身近な例では、海外旅行に行くときの両替です。③たとえば、アメリカに旅行する際に、円をドルに両替します。④これは円を売ってドルを買うということです。⑤昨日は1ドルが106円だったのが、今日は1ドル105円になったりします。⑥相場が変動するので**変動相場制**といい、各先進国が採用しています。

⑦発展途上国の多くは、為替変動がなく安定した**固定相場制**を採用しています。⑧日本も1971年までは1ドル360円の固定相場制でした（p.178参照）。⑨中国はアメリカなどからの要請で「**管理変動相場制**」をとっています。⑩政府管理のもと、一定の為替レートを維持しており、固定相場制から変動相場制に移行する過程にあるといえます。⑪世界の主要国にある**外国為替市場**では、コンピュータや電話で売買取引が行なわれています。⑫為替レートは基本的には外国為替市場の買い手と売り手の**需要と供給のバランス**で決まります。

51. The Causes of Exchange Rate Fluctuations

①Exchange rate fluctuations are caused by purchasing
為替レートの変動   ～によって生じる   購買力平価
power parity, the current-account balance, interest rate,
(←購買する力の等価) 経常収支   金利
and the movement of financial assets.
                     金融資産

②The purchasing power parity is a conversion rate adapted
                                    換算率   適合させた
when exchanging one currency for another. ③It is a state
～を一に変えるとき   水準
where the purchasing power of both currencies is balanced.

④For example, supposing that a Big Mac costs 5.71 dollars in
              ～と仮定すると   かかる
the U.S. and it costs 390 yen in Japan, one dollar has value of

68.4 yen as being calculated by 390/5.71=68.4※. ⑤Although
                                                         ～だけれども
the purchasing power parity is regarded as an indicator of the
                                               目安
long-term exchange rate, it does not reflect the exchange rate
長期的な   反映する
exactly because of too many things and a complicated
正確に   複雑な
distribution system.
流通

⑥The balance of trade influences exchange rates. ⑦For
                        影響する
example, if the export amount exceeds that of the import
          輸出量   上回る   輸出量
amount, companies sell U.S. dollars which they earned from
                                                  稼いだ
the trade, and buy yen. ⑧As a result, the exchange rate of yen
                          その結果

※読み方は、Three hundred and ninety divided by five point seven one equals sixty-eight four.

increases. ⑨If the interest rates of foreign countries are
　　　　　　　　　　金利
higher than that in Japan, people sell yen and buy foreign

currencies. ⑩Consequently, the yen becomes weak. ⑪Also
　　　　　　　その結果として　　円が下がる(→円安になる)　　　　　同様に
the yen becomes weak if Japanese residents deposit money in
　　　　　　　　　　　　　　　　　　　居住者　　　　預金する
a bank abroad or buy expensive financial instruments abroad.

51. 為替レート変動の要因

①為替レートが変動する要因として主に、**購買力平価、貿易の経
常収支、金利、金融資産の動き**などが考えられます。
②購買力平価とは、ある通貨を別の通貨に変えるときの換算比率
の一種です。③それぞれの通貨の購買力が等しくなるような為替
レートの水準です。④たとえば、日本で1個390円のビッグマ
ックがアメリカでは5.71ドルで買えるとすると、390÷5.71で
1ドルが約68.3円になります。⑤購買力平価は為替レートの長
期的な目安になっていますが、実際には無数にあるモノの値段と
複雑な流通のしくみがあるために、単純に為替レートに反映する
わけではありません。
⑥貿易収支は為替レートに影響を与えます。⑦たとえば、日本の
輸出が輸入を上回れば、企業が得たドルを売り、円に換えます。
⑧その結果、円のレートが高くなります。⑨外国の金利が日本よ
りも高ければ、円を売って外国の通貨を買います。⑩したがって、
円安になります。⑪同様に、日本の居住者が海外で預金したり、
高額な金融商品を買ったりすると、円安に傾きます。

52. A Weak Yen and a Strong Yen

①As previously explained, the exchange rate fluctuates
corresponding to various factors. ②When the value of Japanese
yen is lower compared to foreign currency, yen is weak, and
when higher, yen is strong. ③For example, if 1 U.S. dollar was
worth 106 yen yesterday and it is worth 105 yen today, we can
say "the yen got stronger". ④In this case, when we buy a
product of 1 U.S. dollar, it costs 1 yen cheaper than yesterday.
⑤The value of the yen has increased, so this means that the
yen became stronger. ⑥Meanwhile, the value of the U.S. dollar
has decreased, so that the U.S. dollar is weaker.
⑦When the yen is stronger, the Japanese exporters take hits.
⑧Let us assume that a Japanese auto manufacturer sells a
model for 10,000 U.S. dollars in the U.S. ⑨When the
exchange rate is 106 yen to 1 U.S. dollar, it can gain
1,060,000 yen as a sale. ⑩If the exchange rate rises 100 yen
to 1 U.S. dollar, the profit of one car decreases by as much
as 60,000 yen, as the price of one car decreases from

1,060,000 yen to 1,000,000 yen. ⑪In contrast, the importers
逆に 輸入業者

can earn more with exchange gains from the strong yen,
稼ぐ 為替差益の利益

because they purchase goods at lower prices.
購入する

⑫When the yen is weaker, the exporters gain more profit

because they can sell commodities more expensively in
高く

foreign countries.

52. 円安・円高

①前ページで見たように、為替レートはさまざまな要因で変化します。②外国の通貨と比べて、円の価値が下がることを「**円安**」、価値が上がることを「**円高**」といいます。③昨日1ドルが106円だったのに、今日は1ドル105円になったとき、円高になったといいます。④この場合、同じ1ドルの商品を1円安く買えることになります。⑤これは、円の価値が高くなったので、円高というわけです。⑥その一方で、ドルの価値は低くなるので、ドル安になります。

⑦円高になると、輸出関連業者は打撃を受けます。⑧日本の自動車製造販売会社が、アメリカで車を1台1万ドルで売っていたとしましょう。⑨1ドルが106円の頃は106万円で売れていました。⑩しかし、円高で1ドルが100円になるとその車の値段が106万円から100万円に下がり、儲けが6万円少なくなります。⑪逆に、輸入業者は安く仕入れることができ、差益を得ます。⑫円安になると、海外で同じ価格で売っても多くの円が入ってくることになり、輸出業者は利益が増えます。

53. The International Balance of Payments

①The "international balance of payments" is a statistic of the
国際収支 統計
economic trades made between Japan and foreign countries which
経済取引
is systematically compiled. ②It is compiled by the Ministry of
体系的にまとめた 財務省
Finance and the Bank of Japan according to the "Balance of
日本銀行 収支マニュアル
Payment Manual" issued by the IMF (see p.140).

③The balance of payments is divided into three items:
〜に分けられる 項目
current account balance, financial account balance and capital
経常収支 金融収支
transfer account balance. ④The current account balance is the sum
資本移転等収支 合計
of the "trade balance", which is the balance of imports and exports
貿易収支 モノの輸出入
of goods, the "service balance", which is the balance of transactions
サービス収支 取引
not involving the exchange of things such as travel, transportation,
含まない モノのやり取り 輸送
communication, information, and patent royalty fee, the "primary
通信 特許権使用料 第一次所得収支
income balance", which is the balance of income and expenditures
報酬 支出
such as dividends and interest, and the "second income
配当や利子の 第二次所得収支
balance" which is the balance of grant aid such as consumer goods.
無償援助 消費財
⑤The financial account balance is the sales and purchase balance
売買の
of stocks and securities. ⑥Capital transfer account balance is the
株や証券

income and expenditure of free provision of fixed assets, debt
　　　　　　　　　無料提供　　　　　　　固定資産
exemption and transfer of assets due to inheritance.
債務免除　　　　試算の移転　　　　　　相続
⑦In fiscal year 2019, the inbound business was favorable and
2019年度は　　　　　　インバウンド事業　　　　　好調で
the "service balance" was the first profit in the statistics. ⑧The
current account balance was also in the black, 20,599.7
　　　　　　　　　　　　　　　　　　黒字
billion yen, an increase of 4.4% from the previous year.
　　　　　　　　　　　　　　　　　前年

53. 国際収支

①国際収支とは、一定期間内に日本が行なった外国との経済取引を体系的にまとめた統計です。②財務省や日銀が、IMF（p.140参照）の国際収支マニュアルに則って作成します。

③国際収支は、**経常収支**、**金融収支**、**資本移転等収支**の３つの項目に分かれます。④経常収支は、モノの輸出入の収支である「貿易収支」、モノのやり取りをともなわない旅行、輸送、通信、情報、特許権使用料取引などの収支である「サービス収支」、雇用者報酬、配当や利子などの収支による「第一次所得収支」、消費財などの無償援助の収支である「第二次所得収支」の合計です。⑤金融収支は、株や証券の売買収支です。⑥資本移転等収支は、固定資産の無償提供、債務免除や相続に伴う資産の移転等の収支です。

⑦2019年度は、インバウンド事業が順調で、「サービス収支」が統計上初めての黒字となりました。⑧経常収支も20兆597億円の黒字で、前年より4.4%伸びました。

貿易収支が為替レートに影響する
Balance of Trade Influences Exchange Rates

輸出が増えると円高になる
When exports increase, the yen becomes stronger.

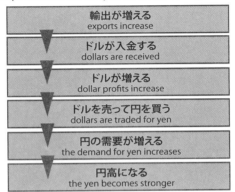

輸出が増える exports increase
ドルが入金する dollars are received
ドルが増える dollar profits increase
ドルを売って円を買う dollars are traded for yen
円の需要が増える the demand for yen increases
円高になる the yen becomes stronger

輸入が増えると円安になる
When imports increase, the yen becomes weaker.

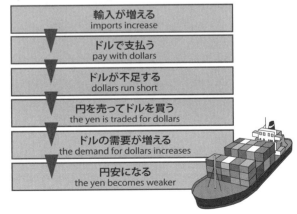

輸入が増える imports increase
ドルで支払う pay with dollars
ドルが不足する dollars run short
円を売ってドルを買う the yen is traded for dollars
ドルの需要が増える the demand for dollars increases
円安になる the yen becomes weaker

為替レート（US ドル / 日本円）の変動

History of the Fluctuation in Dollar to Yen Exchange Rates

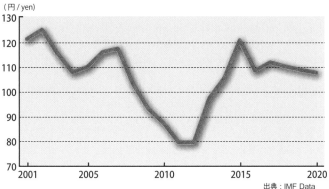

（円 / yen）

出典：IMF Data
source：IMF Data

円高と円安

A Weak Yen and a Strong Yen

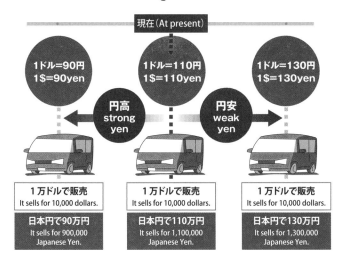

現在（At present）

1ドル=90円
1$=90yen

1ドル=110円
1$=110yen

1ドル=130円
1$=130yen

円高
strong
yen

円安
weak
yen

1万ドルで販売
It sells for 10,000 dollars.

1万ドルで販売
It sells for 10,000 dollars.

1万ドルで販売
It sells for 10,000 dollars.

日本円で90万円
It sells for 900,000
Japanese Yen.

日本円で110万円
It sells for 1,100,000
Japanese Yen.

日本円で130万円
It sells for 1,300,000
Japanese Yen.

54. The World Trade Organization (WTO)

①The World Trade Organization (WTO) is an international
世界貿易機関

organization established to stimulate free trade, in which 164
設立された　　　促進する　自由貿易

countries or areas of the world participate. ②The WTO was
参加する

established in 1995 as a successor to the General Agreement
とって代わるもの　　一般協定

on Tariffs and Trade (GATT). ③GATT was an agreement
関税

concluded in 1948 to prevent the world economy from dividing
締結された　　　　　　　～を―から防ぐ　　分割すること

into economic blocs as in prior to World War 2. ④According to
経済ブロック　　　～にあったように ～より前に　　～によって

this agreement, countries around the world removed the
取り除いた

restrictions on import and reduced tariff rates.
制限　　　　　　　　下げた　関税率

⑤The purpose of the WTO is to determine the rules of trade
目的　　　　　　　　　　　　　決定する

regarding such things as goods, services and intellectual
知的所有権

property so that trade disputes between member countries
～するように 貿易紛争　　　　　　　加盟国

can be resolved. ⑥The two main principles which are
解決される　　　　　　　　原則

imposed on member countries are: the principle of
～に課される

"most-favored nation" treatment by which the tariffs must be
最も優遇された国と同じ待遇　（→最恵国待遇）

imposed under the same condition among the member

countries, and the principle of national treatment by which
内国民待遇

home products and imported products must be treated
国内製品　　　　　　　輸入品

equally. ⑦The WTO holds conferences to gather the member
　　　　　　　　開く　会議　　　　　　集める

countries together for negotiations on trade, which is called
　　　　　　　　　　　交渉

the "round". ⑧However, it is not easy to complete
　　　　　　　　　　　　　　　　　　　　　終える

negotiations among many countries; the Doha round, which

was launched in 2001, has not reached an agreement.
始まった

54. WTO（世界貿易機関）

①WTO（世界貿易機関）は世界中から 164 の国と地域が参加し、自由貿易を促進する国際的な機関です。②WTO は、GATT（関税および貿易に関する一般協定）を発展させた形で 1995 年につくられました。③GATT とは、第 2 次世界大戦以前に世界経済を経済ブロックに分けたこと（ブロック経済）が再び起きないように 1948 年に結ばれた協定です。④この協定により、各国は輸入規制の撤廃と関税率の引き下げを行ないました。

⑤WTO の目的は、モノ、サービス、知的所有権などのやりとりのルールを決め、加盟国間の貿易紛争を解決することです。⑥すべての加盟国に対して関税の条件を同じにすること（最恵国待遇）と、輸入品と国内製品での待遇を変えてはいけない（内国民待遇）という、2 つの原則が課されます。⑦WTO では、各国が一堂に会す「ラウンド」と呼ばれる多国間貿易交渉を開催します。⑧しかし、多数の加盟国の交渉はなかなかまとまらず、2001 年のドーハ・ラウンドの合意は、いまだに得られていません。

55. The Free Trade Agreement (FTA) and the Economic Partner Agreement (EPA)

①In the WTO, negotiations for all member countries did not
交渉

proceed easily because the interests of the participating
進む　　　　　　　　　　利害　　　　　　　　　参加国

countries did not match. ②Accordingly, negotiations mainly
　　　　　　　　　　　　したがって

held between two countries such as a Free Trade
自由貿易協定

Agreement (FTA) and an Economic Partnership Agreement
経済連携協定

(EPA) have become mainstream. ③An FTA is an agreement
主流になってきた

that decides on the elimination or reduction of tariff and non-
撤廃や削減

tariff barriers between two or more countries or regions. ④By

doing so, they aim to expand trade and investment. ⑤An EPA
広げる

is an agreement that creates a wide-ranging cooperation
　　　　　　　　　　　　　　　　　　　　　　　広範囲な　　　　協力体制

system in addition to an FTA, such as deregulation when
　　　　　　～に加えて　　　　　　　　　　　　　規制緩和

people move, improving the investment environment,
　　　　　　　改善すること　　投資環境

supporting bilateral cooperation, and cooperating in the field
　　　　　　　　2国間の協力

of intellectual property. ⑥Japan issued its first EPA with
　　知的財産　　　　　　　　　　　　　　　　発効した

Singapore in November 2002. ⑦As a result, trade and
　　　　　　　　　　　　　　　　　　　　　結果として

investment have expanded, and the number of foreign workers

in specialized fields such as nursing, nursing care, and
　　専門分野　　　　　　　　　　看護　　　　介護

technicians has increased. [8]As of August 2020, Japan has
技師　　　　　　　　　　　　　　2002年8月時点で

FTAs and EPAs with 18 countries and regions (Singapore,
　　　　　　　　　　　　　　　　　　　国と地域

Mexico, Malaysia, Chile, Thailand, Indonesia, Brunei,

ASEAN as a whole, Philippines, Switzerland, Vietnam, India,

Peru, Australia, Mongolia, TPP12[※], TPP11[※], EU) .

55. FTA（自由貿易協定）とEPA（経済連携協定）

①WTO では参加国の利害が一致しないため、全加盟国での交渉がなかなか進みませんでした。②それで **FTA（自由貿易協定）** や **EPA（経済連携協定）** のような主に 2 国間で行われる交渉が主流になりました。③FTA とは、2 国間以上の国家や地域間で関税や非関税障壁の撤廃や削減を決める協定です。④それにより貿易や投資が拡大することを目指します。⑤EPA とは、FTA に加えて、人の移動の際の規制緩和、投資環境の整備、2 国間の協力を後押しし、知的財産分野の協力など、広範囲で協力体制を作る協定のことです。⑥日本は 2002 年 11 月にシンガポールとの間で初の EPA を発効しました。⑦これにより、貿易や投資が拡大し、看護や介護、技師などの専門的分野の外国人労働者の就労も多くなりました。⑧2020 年 8 月時点で、日本は 18 の国や地域（シンガポール，メキシコ，マレーシア，チリ，タイ，インドネシア，ブルネイ，ASEAN 全体，フィリピン，スイス，ベトナム，インド，ペルー，オーストラリア，モンゴル，TPP12[※]，TPP11[※]，EU）と FTA や EPA を締結しています。

※ TPP12 はアメリカを含む TPP 加盟国 12 カ国間での締結、TPP11 はアメリカを除いた
11 カ国間での締結。

56. The Trans-Pacific Partnership (TPP)

①The TPP (Trans-Pacific Partnership Agreement) is a broad-based EPA that aims to liberalize the economies of the Pacific Rim regions. ②In 2006, Singapore, New Zealand, Chile, and Brunei signed the TPSEP (Pacific Trans-Pacific Strategic Economic Partnership Agreement) to completely eliminate tariffs. ③In 2010, the United States, Australia, Peru, Vietnam and Malaysia participated and the TPP expanded. ④Canada and Mexico participated in the negotiations in 2012 and Japan in 2013. ⑤There was some opposition to the participation from the viewpoint of domestic industry protection, but the *Abe* Cabinet decided to participate because it is not premised on "elimination of tariffs without sanctuary".

⑥In February 2016, 12 countries signed (TPP12), but as soon as Trump, who advocated for protectionism, took office as president in January 2017, the United States withdrew from the TPP. ⑧Eleven countries, not including the United States, discussed and reached the CPTPP (Comprehensive and

Advanced Trans-Pacific Partnership Agreement) in March
先進的な

2018 (TPP11). ⑩The areas handled by CPTPP consist of
　　　　　　　　　扱われる　　　　　　　　～からなる

various fields such as financial services, e-commerce,
　　　　　　　　　金融サービス　　　　　　　電子商取引

intellectual property, investment, labor standards and
知的財産　　　　　　　　　　　　　労働基準

environmental standards.
環境基準

56. TPP（環太平洋パートナーシップ協定）

①TPP（環太平洋パートナーシップ協定）とは、環太平洋地域の国々が経済の自由化を目指す、広範囲な EPA です。②2006 年に関税の完全撤廃に向け、シンガポール、ニュージーランド、チリ、ブルネイが TPSEP（環太平洋戦略的経済連携協定）を締結。③2010 年に米国、オーストラリア、ペルー、ベトナム、マレーシアが参加して TPP に拡大。④2012 年にカナダとメキシコ、2013 年に日本が交渉に参加しました。⑤国内産業保護の観点から加入反対の意見もありましたが、「聖域なき関税撤廃」が前提でないことを理由に安倍内閣が参加を決断しました。

⑥2016 年 2 月には、12 カ国が署名しましたが（TPP12）、翌 2017 年 1 月、保護貿易主義を標榜するトランプが大統領に就任するやいなや、米国は TPP から離脱しました。⑦米国を除いた 11 カ国は協議し、2018 年 3 月に CPTPP（包括的及び先進的な環太平洋パートナーシップ協定）を結ぶに至りました（TPP11）。⑧CPTPP で扱われる内容は、金融サービス、電子商取引、知的財産、投資、労働基準や環境基準など多分野からなります。

57.International Monetary Fund (IMF)

①In 1944, the Bretton Woods agreement was signed between
〔ブレトン・ウッズ協定〕 〔締結された〕
the Allied nations in order to secure the economy after World
〔連合国〕 〔安定する〕
War 2. ②In 1946, the International Monetary Fund (IMF)
〔国際通貨基金〕
was established along with the International Bank for
〔設立された〕 〔〜とともに〕 〔国際復興開発銀行〕
Reconstruction and Development (IBRD). ③Subsequently, the
〔続いて〕
General Agreement on Tariffs and Trade (GATT) was signed
〔関税および貿易に関する一般協定〕
in 1947.

④The IMF is operated for the purpose of facilitating
〔〜の目的で〕 〔円滑にすること〕
international transfer of funds and stabilizing exchange rates.
〔移動〕 〔資金〕 〔安定化すること〕〔為替レート〕
⑤In August 2020, 189 countries and territories participated in
〔加盟した〕
the IMF.

⑥The activities of the IMF are supervising, money lending and
〔活動〕 〔監視〕 〔融資〕
technical support. ⑦The IMF supervises member countries'
〔技術援助〕 〔監視する〕
monetary policy and makes policy recommendations. ⑧It also
〔金融政策〕 〔政策の提言〕
provides financial assistance to financially distressed countries
〔提供する〕 〔財政がひっ迫している〕
in crisis and low-income countries. ⑨Additionally, it provides
〔危機的状況で〕〔低所得の〕 〔また〕
technical support and human resource development to countries
〔人材〕 〔開発〕

which are poor in the knowledge of economic and
　　　　　～が不足している　　　　知識
monetary policy.

⑩The IMF aims to improve the living standards of member
　　　　　　　目指す　　　　　　　生活水準
countries cooperating with the World Bank, which is also an
　　　　　　　～と連携して　　　世界銀行
organization in the United Nations system.
組織　　　　　　　国際連合機関

57. IMF（国際通貨基金）

①1944 年、連合国の間で戦後の経済を安定させることを目的として、ブレトン・ウッズ協定が結ばれました。②この協定により、1946 年に IMF（国際通貨基金）と IBRD（国際復興開発銀行）が設立されました。③さらに、1947 年には GATT（関税および貿易に関する一般協定）が締結されました。

④IMF は国際的な資金の移動を円滑化し、為替レートの安定を図ることを目的に活動しています。⑤加盟国は 2020 年 8 月の時点で 189 の国と地域です。

⑥IMF の主な活動は「監視」、「資金融資」、「技術援助」の 3 つです。

⑦IMF は加盟国の金融政策を監視したり、政策の提言をします。

⑧財政的に苦しくて危機に陥っている国や低所得の国に資金援助を行ないます。⑨また、経済・金融政策の知識が不足している国へは技術援助や人材育成を行ないます。

⑩IMF は、同じく国際連合の専門機関である世界銀行と連携して、加盟国の生活水準の向上を目指しています。

58. The Postwar Economy in the United States

①After World War 1 and 2, the economy of the U.S. was booming and it possessed the greatest amount of gold in the
急成長した　保有した　もっとも多くの〜
world. ②The U.S. dollar became the key currency (see p.122)
基軸通貨
because, under the Bretton Woods system, the U.S. promised
約束した
an exchange of approximately 35 dollars per 1 ounce of gold
約　　　　　　　　　　　　　　　　〜につき
on the security of gold in possession.
〜の保証として　所有している金
③In postwar U.S.A., where demand was increasing consistent
戦後の　　　　　需要　　　　　　　　　〜とともに
with the improvement of the standards of living, and supply
向上　　　　　　　　水準　　　　　供給
was increasing corresponding to the mass production
〜にともなって起きる　大量生産
accomplished by technology innovation, the economy grew
なし遂げられた　技術革新
steadily. ④Consequently, the U.S. economy marked a golden
順調に　　その結果　　　　　　　　　迎えた　黄金時代
age in the 1960s.

⑤After Lyndon Johnson took office in 1963, the military
大統領に就任した　　　軍事介入
intervention in Vietnam expanded. ⑥As the war situation
拡大した
deteriorated, antiwar campaigns and antiracism activities
悪化した　反戦運動　　　　人種差別反対運動
occurred domestically, which became social problems.
起こった　国内では　　　　　　社会問題
⑦President Johnson adopted the Great Society policy to
採用した　偉大な社会政策

deal with the social problems in order to enrich the social
　解決する　　　　　　　　　　　　　　　　　　強化する
welfare.
福祉

58. 米国の戦後経済

①第1次・第2次世界大戦を経て、アメリカ経済は大きく成長し、世界最大の金（きん）保有国となりました。②ブレトン・ウッズ体制下で、この金を裏づけとして、1オンスの金を約35ドルと交換することを約束したことから、米ドルは**基軸通貨**（p.122 参照）になりました。

③戦後のアメリカは、国民の生活向上により、需要が増加するとともに、技術革新による大量生産で供給が増え、順調に経済成長を続けていました。④そして、1960年代にアメリカ経済は黄金時代を迎えました。

⑤1963年にリンドン・ジョンソンが大統領に就任すると、ベトナムへの軍事介入が拡大しました。⑥ベトナム戦争が激化するにつれ、アメリカ国内では反戦運動と人種差別反対運動が活発になり、大きな社会問題となりました。⑦ジョンソン大統領はこれに対処するため、「偉大な社会」政策をとり、社会福祉の充実を図りました。

59. Nixon Shock

①The government expenditure for defense costs and welfare
<u>財政支出</u>　　　<u>防衛</u>　　　　<u>福祉</u>

costs under President Johnson increased the government
<u>増加させた</u>

budget deficit. ②This resulted in stagflation in which
<u>財政赤字</u>　　　　<u>結果として〜になった</u>　<u>スタグフレーション</u>

economic conditions become worse, while there was an
<u>景気</u>　　　　　　　　　　　<u>一方で</u>

increase in the prices of goods and services, in the 1970s.

③The quantity of Gold possessed by the U.S. became
<u>量</u>　　　　　　<u>保有されている</u>

insufficient for the currency circulation as the government
<u>不十分な</u>　　　　<u>通貨発行高</u>

expenditures increased because of the defense costs for the
<u>支出</u>

Vietnam war and the social welfare costs for the Great

Society policy. ④Consequently, the market, expecting a
<u>このことから</u>　　　　　　　<u>〜を予測して</u>

devaluation of the U.S. dollar, sold the U.S. dollar and bought
<u>切り下げ</u>

ダッチマーク
the Japanese yen and Deutschmark.
<u>ドイツマルク</u>

⑤In 1971, with the declining value of the U.S. dollar,
<u>下落している</u>　<u>価値</u>

President Nixon declared an end to the direct convertibility
<u>宣言した</u>　　　　　　　<u>直接兌換</u>

of the dollar to gold. ⑥Accordingly, the Bretton Woods
<u>これによって</u>

system collapsed and the fixed exchange rate system ended.
<u>崩壊した</u>　　　<u>(通貨の)固定相場制</u>

⑦This economic policy implemented by Richard Nixon was
<u>実行された</u>

called "The Nixon Shock". ⑧During the period following
　　　　　　　　　　　　　その期間ずっと　　　　　　　　　　　この後の

this, inflation continued.

1971
1 $ = ¥360

59. ニクソン・ショック
＊＊＊＊＊＊＊＊＊＊＊＊＊＊＊＊＊

①ジョンソン大統領が推し進めた軍事費と福祉の財政支出は、財政赤字を増やしました。②その結果、1970年に入ると、「物価が上昇しているのに景気が悪くなる」というスタグフレーションが起こります。

③ベトナム戦争の軍事費と「偉大な社会」政策の福祉で、財政赤字が増大したことにより、アメリカの金の保有量が通貨発行高に対して不足しました。④このことから、市場ではドルの切り下げが行なわれると予測し、ドルを売り、円やマルクを買う動きが活発化しました。

⑤ドルの価値が下落を始めたことから、1971年、ニクソン大統領がドル紙幣と金との兌換停止を宣言しました。⑥これにより、ブレトン・ウッズ体制は崩壊し、通貨の固定相場制は終わりました。⑦ニクソンが行なったこの経済政策は**ニクソン・ショック**と呼ばれています。⑧その後、アメリカではインフレが続きます。

60. Neoliberalism

①Neoliberalism is a way of thinking that the service of the nation to the people is reduced and the market principle is emphasized. ②Until the 1970s, the economic policies of developed countries were based on Keynesian economics, and they aimed to be a "large government" in which the nation guaranteed individual rights and nationalized major industries with the aim of enhancing social security. ③The oil crisis of the 1970s triggered stagnation and the economy of developed countries slowed down. ④In the 1980s, there was criticism that the cause of the economic stagnation was the expanded government and the government's intervention in the economy. ⑤What attracted attention was neoliberalism, which was advocated by Friedman and aimed at a "small government." ⑥A politician who is known to have aggressively carried out neoliberal policies is British Prime Minister Margaret Thatcher. ⑦Britain, which has emphasized social welfare, suffered from the economic downturn during the 1960s and

146

1970s. ⑧Thatcher overcame this by privatizing state-owned
克服した　　　　　　　　　　　　民営化　　　　　　国営公共事業

public works, reducing income tax, introducing consumption
　　　　　　引下げ　　所得税　　　導入　　　　　消費税

tax, and so on. ⑨In Japan, Prime Minister *Nakasone* and Prime
　　　　　　　　　　　　　　　　　中曽根首相

Minister *Koizumi* have taken the neoliberal route. ⑩However,
小泉首相　　　　　　　　　　　　　　　　　路線

it tends to be advantageous to large companies, and the side
　　　　　　　　　有利である　　　　大企業　　　　　　　副作用

effect of widening disparity is becoming a problem.
　　　　格差拡大

60. 新自由主義

①**新自由主義**とは、国家の国民に対するサービスを縮小し、市場原理を重視する考え方です。②1970年代まで、先進国の経済政策はケインズ経済学を基本とし、社会保障の充実を目指し主要産業を国有化するなど、国家が個人の権利を保障する「大きな政府」を目指していました。③1970年代の石油危機を契機に先進諸国の経済は停滞しました。④1980年代になると、経済停滞の原因は政府の肥大化と、政府の経済への介入にあるという批判が起こりました。⑤そこで注目されたのが、フリードマンらが提唱し、「小さな政府」を目指す新自由主義でした。

⑥積極的に新自由主義政策を行ったことで知られる政治家は、イギリスのサッチャー首相です。⑦社会福祉を重視してきたイギリスは、1960〜70年代に経済の低迷に悩まされました。⑧サッチャーは、国営公共事業の民営化、所得税減税、消費税の導入などで、これを克服しました。⑨日本では、中曽根首相、小泉首相らが新自由主義路線を取りました。⑩しかし、大企業に有利になりがちなため、その副作用である格差拡大が問題になっています。

61. Reaganomics

①President Reagan, who took office in 1981, implemented an
就任した   実施した
economic policy, Reaganomics, and extended tax reductions,
                 レーガノミクス   伸展させた   減税
loosened regulations, effected high-interest policies, and
規制緩和   達成した   高金利
expanded the military. ②This policy pulled the U.S. economy
拡張した   軍備   引っぱり出した
out of inflation which had been ongoing from 1970.
～から   続いている
③Meanwhile, the defense costs and the reduction of taxes
その一方で   国防費   減税
increased the government budget deficit and the exchange
増大した   財政赤字   為替レート
rate of the U.S. dollar fell at the same time. ④That was
known as the "Twin Deficits".
           双子の赤字
⑤In 1985, the U.S. government was determined to intervene
                              決心した   ～に介入する
in the foreign exchange market to strengthen the Japanese
   外国為替市場   強くする
yen against the U.S. dollar. ⑥A conference of Ministers and
                            先進5カ国蔵相・中央銀行総裁会議
Governors of the Group of Five which included Japan, signed
                                                   調印した
the Plaza Accord, an agreement to depreciate the U.S. dollar,
プラザ合意   合意   価値を下げる
after which the exchange rate of the Japanese yen fell
           為替レート
quickly.
⑦In 1986, in order to counteract the high-yen recession,
          ～するために 解消する   円高不況

148

the Bank of Japan reduced the official discount rate. ⑧This
日本銀行　　　　　　　　引き下げた　公定歩合

triggered the bubble economy of Japan (see p.184).
引き金になった　バブル経済

Reaganomics

61. レーガノミクス

①1981 年に就任したレーガン大統領は、**レーガノミクス**という
経済政策を実施し、減税、規制緩和、高金利政策、軍備拡張を進
めました。②この政策により、アメリカは 1970 年から続いたイ
ンフレから脱出しました。

③しかしその一方で、軍事費増大や減税などで財政赤字が増大し、
同時に US ドルの為替レートが下がり（ドル高）、貿易赤字が増
大しました。④いわゆる「**双子の赤字**」です。

⑤1985 年、米国は外国為替市場に介入して、US ドルに対して
日本円を高くすることを決定しました。⑥日本を含む G5（先進
5 カ国蔵相・中央銀行総裁会議）で、「ドル安」を推進する決定（**プ
ラザ合意**）が行なわれた後、円の為替レートは急激に下がり、円
高になりました。

⑦1986 年になって、日本では円高不況から脱却するために、日
銀が公定歩合を引き下げました。⑧これが日本の**バブル経済**の始
まり（p.184 参照）となりました。

62. The Globalization

①After 1989 when the Cold War ended, free trade and
democracy extended to the world in a process now called
globalization, which was advanced under the initiative of the
U.S., a supercountry. ②Even the former Soviet bloc and
China were brought into global capitalism, and the market
framework, dominated by the U.S. dollar, was established.
③In the 1980s in the U.S., many investment funds were
established, where money was collected from people and
companies, and invested. ④Moreover, hedge funds, a type of
investment fund, were founded. ⑤Hedge funds manage
portfolios made up of financial instruments, such as stocks
and foreign exchanges, and derivatives, such as futures and
options. ⑥They repeatedly trade a large amount of financial
instruments worldwide in the short term in order to make a
profit irrespective of the fluctuation of market rates, so that
they have a profound effect on the economies of countries
around the world. ⑦On the other hand, the number of M&A

by large companies has increased rapidly. ⑧Large companies

compete to acquire companies around the world and become
　　　　　〜することを競う　獲得する

multinational corporations. ⑨These multinational corporations
多国籍企業

can move funds and goods beyond borders freely. ⑩Globalization
　　　　　　　　　　　　国境を越えて

is progressing gradually as represented by the movement of
進んでいる　　　徐々に　　代表される

hedge funds and multinational corporations.

62. グローバル化

①1989年、冷戦が終結し、超大国である米国の主導で**グローバル化**が進み、自由貿易と民主主義が世界に広がりました。②旧ソ連圏や中国もグローバル資本主義に組み込まれ、ドルによる市場体制が整いました。

③1980年代の米国では、個人や企業からお金を集めて運用する**投資ファンド**が多く設立されました。④さらに、投資ファンドの一種である**ヘッジファンド**が登場します。⑤ヘッジファンドは、株や外国為替などの金融商品に、先物取引やオプションなどの金融派生商品をセットにして運用します。⑥相場の上下に連動せず収益を上げることを目的として、短期的に大量の金融商品の売買をくり返すので、ヘッジファンドは世界経済に大きな影響を及ぼします。⑦一方で、1990年頃から企業買収が急増しました。⑧大企業は競って世界の企業を吸収合併して、多国籍企業となりました。⑨多国籍企業は、自社の利益のために国境を越えて資金や物資を動かすことができます。⑩これらヘッジファンドや多国籍企業の動きに代表されるように、グローバリゼーションが徐々に進行していきました。

63. The Subprime Lending and the Global Economic Crisis

①In the U.S. in the 1990s, the IT industry developed, which
　　　　　　　　　　　　　　　IT産業
caused the dot-com bubble economy to emerge in the late
　　　　ITバブル経済　　　　　　　　　　　現われる
1990s. ②However this bubble collapsed in 2000. ③The
　　　　　　　　　　　　崩壊した
chairman of the Federal Reserve Board (FRB), Alan
議長　　　　　連邦準備制度
Greenspan, tried to stimulate the economy by decreasing
　　　　　　　　　刺激する　　　　　　　　　引き下げ
short-term interest rates and reducing taxes to prevent the
短期の　　金利　　　　　　減税　　　　　防ぐ
same economic crisis as in Japan. ④As a result, mortgage
　　　　　　危機　　　　　　　　　　　　　住宅ローン
loans as typified by subprime loans increased and it became
　　　～に代表される　サブプライム・ローン
easy for people with low-incomes to purchase houses.
　　　　　　　　低所得の　　　　　購入する
⑤Correspondingly, housing prices started to rise and the
　それに応じて　　　　　　　　　　　　　上昇する
housing bubble emerged. ⑥A subprime loan is a high-
住宅バブル　　　　　　　　　　　　　　　　　高金利
interest loan for people with poor credit using their house and
　　　　　　　　　　　信用があまりない
real estate as collateral. ⑦These subprime loans were sold to
不動産　　担保として
brokerage firms and investment banks as securities, which
証券会社　　　　　　投資銀行　　　　証券として
were built into funds and sold to investors.
～に組み込まれた
⑧In 2007, sales of houses declined and real-estate prices
　　　　　売上げ　　　　　減少した
started to fall. ⑨Consequently, subprime lending collapsed
　　　　　　　そのため

and, Lehman Brothers[※], which <u>owned</u> large amounts of
　　　　　　　　　　　　　　保有した
<u>subprime</u> <u>securities</u>, <u>went bankrupt</u>. ⑩<u>Subsequently</u>, <u>as</u>
　　　　　証券　　　　倒産した　　　　　　　　続いて　　　　　　　　〜のため
<u>financial institutions</u> around the world sold stocks, stock
金融機関
prices collapsed and this <u>triggered</u> a world financial
　　　　　　　　　　　　きっかけになった　　世界金融危機
<u>crisis</u> <u>along with</u> a <u>worldwide recession</u>.
　　　　〜に加えて　　　世界同時不況

63. サブプライム問題と世界金融危機

①1990年代に米国ではIT産業が発展し、後半には**ITバブル**になりました。②このバブルは2000年に崩壊します。③連邦準備制度のグリーンスパン議長は、日本の二の舞にならないよう、短期金利の引き下げと減税によって、経済の活性化を図りました。④その結果、サブプライム・ローンに代表される住宅ローンが増え、低所得者が簡単に住宅を手に入れるようになりました。⑤2002年頃から住宅価格が高騰し、**住宅バブル**が起こりました。⑥サブプライム・ローンとは、返済できる信用度の低い人たち向けの高金利ローンで、その家や土地が担保になっています。⑦また、その債権を証券化して証券会社や投資銀行に販売され、これが金融商品に組み込まれ、投資家に売られました。⑧2007年に入ると、住宅が売れなくなり、不動産価格が下落を始めました。⑨そのため、サブプライム・ローンは破綻し、その証券を多く保有していたリーマン・ブラザーズ[※]が倒産しました。⑩これを受け、世界の金融機関が現金を確保するために株を売ったことから、株価が暴落し、世界金融危機、世界同時不況に突入しました。

※ リーマン・ブラザーズ：当時、米国第4位の大手投資銀行。

64. ASEAN's Economy

①ASEAN (Association of Southeast Asian Nations) is an organization established in 1967 by five countries, Indonesia, Malaysia, Philippines, Singapore and Thailand, aiming at economic cooperation and political stability. ②Later, 5 countries, Brunei, Vietnam, Myanmar, Laos and Cambodia joined. ③Japan has built close cooperation with ASEAN as a business partner since Prime Minister *Fukuda* attended the ASEAN Summit Meeting held in Kuala Lumpur in 1977. ④The East Asia Summit has been held once a year since 2005 to discuss strengthening economic partnerships and issues in each country concerned. ⑤Participating countries are the 10 ASEAN countries, Japan, China, South Korea, Australia, New Zealand, India, USA and Russia.

⑥ASEAN countries established the "ASEAN Economic Community (AEC)" in November 2015. ⑦The 10 member countries have established one economic zone, in which tariffs on goods have almost disappeared, and various

standards have been <u>unified</u>. ⑧As of 2018, the AEC has a
　　　　　　　　　　　　統一された
規格

total population of more than 650 million, making it a larger

market than the EU.

64. アジアの経済

①**ASEAN**（東南アジア諸国連合）とは、1967 年にインドネシア、マレーシア、フィリピン、シンガポール、タイの５カ国が、経済協力や政治の安定を目指して設立した組織です。②のちにブルネイ、ベトナム、ミャンマー、ラオス、カンボジアの５ヵ国が加盟しました。③日本は 1977 年にクアラルンプールで開催された ASEAN 首脳会議に福田首相が出席して以来、ASEAN とはビジネスパートナーとして緊密な協力関係を築いています。④2005 年から毎年１回、東アジア首脳会議が開催され、経済連携の強化や、関係各国の課題について協議しています。⑤参加国は、ASEAN10 カ国、日本、中国、韓国、オーストラリア、ニュージーランド、インド、米国、ロシアです。

⑥ASEAN 諸国は、2015 年 11 月に「**ASEAN 経済共同体（AEC）**」を創設しました。⑦加盟 10 カ国は一つの経済圏となり、域内の物品関税がほぼなくなり、さまざまな規格が統一されています。⑧2018 年時点で、AEC の総人口は 6 億 5,000 万人を超え、EU よりも大きな規模の市場となっています。

65. The European Union Economy

①European countries have repeated wars over resources.
資源をめぐり

②Germany, France, Italy, the Netherlands, and Luxembourg signed the Paris Treaty in 1951 for the purpose of avoiding
～を目的に　　　　　避けること
this and jointly managing coal and iron ore. ③The European
石炭　　鉄鋼
Coal and Steel Community (ECSC) was established in 1952.
設立した

④This evolved and the EU (European Union) was established
発展した
in 1993. ⑤In 2002, the distribution of the unified currency
供給　　　　　　　統一通貨
"Euro" began, and the movement of people and goods in the
ユーロ　　　　　移動　　　　　　　　　　　　域内で
region was liberalized. ⑥In the latter half of the 2000s, it
自由化した
became clear that the German economy was the only success.

⑦The eurozone was upset due to the Greek financial crisis
ユーロ圏　　動揺した　～のために
since 2012 and the influx of refugees resulting since 2015 from
流入　　難民
the civil war in Syria. ⑧The United Kingdom has continued to
内戦
use its own currency, the pound, even though it joined the EC
独自通貨　　　　　ポンド
in 1973. ⑨With the rapid increase in immigrants from Eastern
急増　　　　　　移民
European countries, which had become members of the EU,
the anti-EU faction became more powerful in Britain. ⑩In
UE離脱派

the 2016 referendum asking whether to withdraw from or
　　　　国民投票　　　　　　　　　　　　　　　　脱退する
remain in the EU, the anti-EU faction won by a narrow
残留する　　　　　　　　　　　　　　　　　　　　僅差で
margin. ⑪After that, the pro-EU faction and the anti-EU
　　　　　　　　　　　　　　残留派
faction confronted each other and the chaos continued, but in
　　　　対立した　　　　　　　　　　　混乱
January 2020 the UK officially withdraw from the EU.
　　　　　　　　　　　　　正式に　　脱退した

65. EU の経済

①ヨーロッパ諸国は資源をめぐる戦争をくり返してきました。
②これを避け、石炭と鉄鋼を共同管理することを目的として、
1951 年、ドイツ、フランス、イタリア、オランダ、ルクセンブ
ルグがパリ条約に調印。③1952 年に欧州石炭鉄鋼共同体(ECSC)
が設立されました。④これが発展し、1993 年に EU（欧州連合）
が発足しました。⑤2002 年に統一通貨の「ユーロ」の流通が
始まり、域内で、人と物の移動の自由化が進みました。⑥2000
年代後半になると、ドイツ経済の一人勝ちが明確になりました。
⑦2012 年からのギリシャの財政危機や、2015 年以降のシリア
内戦に起因する難民の流入から、ユーロ圏に動揺が起こりました。
⑧イギリスは、1973 年の EC 加盟以降、独自通貨であるポンド
を使用し続けました。⑨EU に加盟した東欧からの移民が急増す
ると、イギリス国内では、EU 離脱派が勢力を強めました。⑩2016
年に行われた EU 離脱・残留を問う国民投票で、EU 離脱派が僅
差で勝利しました。⑪その後も残留派と離脱派が対立して混乱が
続きましたが、2020 年 1 月に正式に EU から離脱しました。

66. China's Economy

①In China, Deng Xiaoping promoted the "Chinese economic reform" in 1978, and since then China has continued to achieve sustained high growth. ②Although being a socialist country, China accepted foreign direct investment, opened up the domestic market, and recorded a double-digit economic growth rate from 2003 to 2007. ③In 2010, China became an economic power with the second largest GDP in the world (2011 GDP per capita was 90th in the world). ④The reason for the rapid growth is that cheap labor force is abundant, exports have grown due to the low exchange rate of the yuan, and the trade surplus has increased.

⑤Since 2010, IT-related high-tech industries such as Huawei and Alibaba have grown rapidly, and China has transformed from "a factory in the world" into "a huge market" attracting investments from around the world. ⑥In foreign policies, President Xi Jinping adopted the "Belt and Road Initiative", in which China has been making strategic investments in countries in the Asian-Pacific, Europe and Africa, which has

strengthened China's influence. ⑦On the other hand, conflicts

　強めた　　　　　　　　　　　　　　一方で　　　　　　対立

with Western countries are becoming more serious due to

negative aspects such as intellectual property rights

否定的な側面　　　　　　　　　　知的財産権

infringement, repression of minorities, and conflict with

侵害　　　　　抑圧　　　　　少数民族

neighboring countries due to military expansion.

軍事的緊張

66. 中国の経済

①中国では、1978年に鄧小平（とうしょうへい）が**改革開放政策**を推し進め、以来、持続的な高度成長を続けています。②社会主義国でありながら、外国からの直接投資を受け入れ、国内市場を開放した中国は、2003〜2007年には2ケタの経済成長率を記録しました。③2010年には、GDPが世界第2位の経済大国になりました（国民1人当たりの2011年のGDPは世界第90位）。④急成長の理由は、安価な労働力が豊富なこと、人民元の為替レートが低いため輸出が伸び、貿易黒字が増えたことなどです。

⑤2010年以降は、ファーウエイ、アリババなどのIT系ハイテク産業が急成長し、「世界の工場」から「世界からの投資を呼び込む巨大市場」へと変貌を遂げました。⑥習近平国家主席は、対外的に**一帯一路政策**をとり、アジア太平洋、欧州、アフリカなどに戦略的投資を行い、影響力を強めました。

⑦その一方で、知的財産権の侵害、少数民族の弾圧、軍事的膨張による周辺諸国との軋轢といった負の側面から、欧米諸国との対立が深刻化しています。

67. US-China trade war

①Since 2000, China, which has seen remarkable economic growth,
著しい
has started to become a developed power after the Beijing Olympics
先進大国　　　　　　　　　　　北京五輪
in 2008 and the Shanghai World Expo in 2010. ②The largest trade
上海万博　　　　　　　　　　　　　　　　最大貿易相手国
partner of China has long been the United States. ③The US trade
deficit with China has continued to expand since 1985, reaching 419
貿易赤字　　　　　　　　　　　　拡大する
billion dollars in 2018. ④When President Trump took office in 2017,
トランプ大統領　　　就任した
he began to take policy measures to eliminate the trade deficit with
政策　　　　　　　解消する
China. ⑤Starting in 2018, additional taxation on steel products was
2018年以降　　　追加関税
begun, and the tariff rate on industrial robots and semiconductors
関税率　　　　産業用ロボット　　　　半導体
imported from China has been greatly increased since then. ⑥At
the end of 2018, there was a retaliatory battle where the United
報復的な争い
States imposed tariffs on almost half of Chinese products and China
関税を課した
imposed tariffs on about 70% of American products. ⑦After that,
through direct talks between President Trump and President Xi
Jinping and through U.S.-China trade talks, mutual concessions
米中貿易協議　　　　　　　相互譲歩
have been sought, but the issue of trade friction has not been
貿易摩擦問題
dispelled. ⑧Due to the rise of China in recent years in the field of
～のために 台頭

high-tech technology and tensions with neighboring countries over
ハイテク技術　　　　　緊張　　　　　周辺諸国

maritime expansion, confrontation between the United States and
海洋進出　　　　　対立

China extends not only to economic but also to military
広がる　　〜だけでなく…へも　　　　　　　　軍事面

aspects. ⑨There is also a view that the battle for hegemony of the
見方　　　　覇権争い

world by the United States and China would be the beginning of

a "new cold war state".
新冷戦状態

67. 米中貿易戦争

①2000 年以降、経済成長が著しい中国は、2008 年の北京五輪、2010 年の上海万博を経て、先進大国に踊り出ました。②中国最大の貿易相手国は長い間米国でした。③米国の対中貿易赤字は 1985 年以降拡大を続け、2018 年には 4190 億ドルになりました。④2017 年にトランプ大統領が就任すると、対中貿易赤字を解消する政策手段に出ました。⑤2018 年以降、鉄鋼製品などへの追加課税に始まり、その後も中国から輸入される産業用ロボットや半導体の関税率は大きく引上げられました。⑥2018 年の終わりには、アメリカが中国製品のほぼ半分、中国はアメリカ製品の約 7 割に関税をかけるという報復合戦の様相を呈しました。⑦その後トランプ大統領と習近平国家主席の直接会談や米中貿易協議による互いの譲歩が模索されましたが、今も貿易摩擦問題は払拭されていません。⑧近年の中国にみるハイテク技術分野における台頭や海洋進出をめぐる周辺諸国との緊張などにより、米中の対立は経済面のみならず軍事面にも及んでいます。⑨こうした米中両国による世界の覇権争いを「新冷戦状態」に突入したとする見方もあります。

Inflation Targeting 　インフレ目標値

①Inflation targeting is an economic policy in which a central bank determines a target inflation rate. ②The central bank attempts to steer actual inflation towards the target through the use of interest rate changes and other monetary tools. ③When interest rates are higher, people and companies are reluctant to lend money, so that the inflation rate tends to be inversely related. ④The central bank raises the interest rate when inflation appears to be above the target. ⑤In contrast, the central bank lowers the interest rate when inflation appears to be below the target. ⑥When the interest rate is almost zero as in Japan, the central bank adjusts the money supply instead of the interest rate to control inflation. ⑦The central bank issues more money when the inflation rate appears to be below the target, and issues less money when the inflation rate appears to be above the target. ⑧Therefore inflation targeting allows the economy to stabilize.

①インフレターゲットとは、中央銀行がインフレ率の数値目標を定める政策です。②中央銀行は金利の変更など金融手段を使って、インフレ率が目標値に向かうように誘導します。③金利が上がると、個人も会社もお金を借りたがらなくなるので、金利とインフレ率は反比例する傾向にあります。④そこで中央銀行は、インフレ率が目標値より上がると、中央銀行金利を上げます。⑤逆にインフレ率が目標値よりも下がると、金利を下げます。⑥日本のように金利がほとんどゼロの場合には、中央銀行は貨幣の流通量を調整してインフレ率を制御します。
⑦中央銀行は、インフレ率が目標値よりも低い場合には貨幣の発行量を増やし、インフレ率が目標値より低いときには貨幣の発行量を減らします。⑧このようにして、インフレターゲットを定めることにより、経済を安定させることができます。

Abenomics

Chapter 6

History of Japanese Economy

第6章

日本経済の歴史

68. The Economic Policy of the New *Meiji* Government

①In the first year of the *Meiji* Era in Japan, more than 70 percent
明治時代

of the people at work were engaged in agricultural and forestry
～に従事した　　　　　農林業

industries, and more than 60 percent of the production was
生産物

agricultural produce. ②In order to oppose the great western
対抗する　欧米列強

powers and maintain independence, as an agricultural country,
維持する　独立

the Japanese government put into action the "encouragement of
実施した　　　　　殖産興業

new industry" policy. ③The government introduced industries
導入した

and technology from the western countries, built various
技術

government-run model factories and developed national mines.
官営模範工業　　　　　　　　　　開発した　　国営の鉱山

④It gave privileges to some private entrepreneurs such as *Mitsui*
特権　　　　　　　民間の　企業家

and *Mitsubishi*, who were called "political contractors".
政商

⑤Although many Asian countries were colonized by the great
植民地化された

western powers one after another, Japan promoted military
次々に　　　　　　　　　推し進めた

industries and enhanced their military powers under the slogan
強化した　　　　　　　　　　　　　　　標語

"increasing wealth and military power". ⑥In order to secure the
富国強兵　　　　　　　　　　　　　　　確保する

governmental treasury funds, "land tax reforms" were
財政資金　　　　　　　地租改正

implemented. ⑦Once the farmers were able to own land, a land-
実施された　　一度～すると

tax was imposed upon on them, and they were drawn into a cash
　　　　課された　　　　　　　　　　　　　　　～に引き込まれた

economy. ⑧The *Meiji* government was financially strapped
　　　　　　　　　　　　　　　　　　　　　　財政的に　苦しかった

because they had fought two civil wars, the *Boshin* War and
　　　　　　　　　　　　　　　内戦　　　　　戊辰戦争

the *Seinan* War. ⑨In 1876, the Lord of the Treasury at that
西南戦争　　　　　　　　　　　大蔵卿

time, *Ohkuma Shigenobu* issued fiat money to cover
　　　　　　　　　　　　　発行した　不換紙幣　　　補う

expenditures, however, this caused rampant inflation.
費用　　　　　　　　　　　　　　　　　激しい

68. 明治新政府の経済政策

①明治初年の日本では、有業者の7割以上が農林業に従事し、生産物の6割以上は農産物でした。②農業国日本が列強に対抗し独立を維持するために、政府が実施したのが「**殖産興業**」政策です。③西洋の産業や技術を導入し、さまざまな**官営模範工場**を作り、直営の鉱山を開発しました。④三井や三菱といった特定の民間事業家には特権が与えられ、**政商**と呼ばれました。⑤欧米列強がアジアの国々を次々に植民地化していくなか、政府は「**富国強兵**」のもとに軍需産業を興し、軍備を拡張しました。⑥政府の財政資金を確保するためには、**地租改正**が実施されました。⑦農民は土地を所有できるようになると同時に、地租の金納が義務づけられて、貨幣経済の波に巻き込まれていきました。
⑧明治政府は戊辰戦争や西南戦争などの内戦に費やした巨額の軍費支出によって、財政がひっ迫していました。⑨1876年に、当時の大蔵卿・大隈重信は不換紙幣を発行してこれを補おうとしますが、結果、激しいインフレになりました。

①The next Lord of the Treasury, *Matsukata Masayoshi*
　　　　　　大蔵卿

adopted an austerity policy to control inflation and collect
採用した　　緊縮財政　　　　　　　抑制する　　　　　　　回収する

money which lost value. ②The government sold national
　　　　　　　　　　　　　　　　　　　　　　　　官営の

factories and mines in deficit to private companies such as
工場　　　　　鉱山　　赤字の　　民間の

political contractors and increased tax rates, so that the
政商　　　　　　　　　　　　　　　　　　　　　　　　　～になるように

revenues could cover the expenditures.
蔵入　　　　　　　　　　歳出

③In 1882, the Bank of Japan was established in order to collect
　　　　　　日本銀行

the fiat money and control the money centrally. ④Subsequently,
不換紙幣　　　　　　　　　　　　　　　中心に(→1カ所に)　その後

silver certificate money was issued which could be exchanged
銀兌換紙幣　　　　　　　　　　　　　　　　　　　　　　交換される

for a certain amount of silver. ⑤As a result of reducing the
　　　一定量の　　　　　　　　　　～の結果として　減少

money supply, rampant deflation occurred, and the price of
　　　　　　　激しい　　　　　　　起きた

agricultural products fell quickly, which in turn increased the
農作物　　　　　　　　　　　　　　　　　　　次に

number of farmers who went and found work in the city.

⑥As the stability of commodity prices and low interest rates
　　　安定　　　　　　　　　　　　　　　　低利率

and the working class developed which were brought about
　　　労働者階級　　　　　　　　　　もたらされた

by the "*Matsukata* Deflation", the "increase of business
　　　松方デフレ　　　　　　　企業勃興

enterprises", in other words, a boom to establish companies,

occurred. ⑦A large amount of funds were needed to establish
多額の　　　　　　　　　　　　資金
railroad companies and thread manufacturing companies.
紡績
⑧In such cases, the companies made use of a system called
活用した
"stock collateral loan", in which a shareholder could borrow
〜を担保にした　　　　　　　　　　　　　　　　　　　　貸付を受ける
money from banks to buy stocks on the security of the
担保
company's shares.

69. 日本の産業革命①

①次の大蔵卿・松方正義は、緊縮財政方針をとって、価値の下落した紙幣の回収を行ない、激化するインフレの鎮静に努めました。
②また政府は、赤字の続く官営工場や直轄鉱山を政商などの民間に払い下げ、増税し、蔵入確保を目指しました。
③1882年、不換紙幣を回収し、お札の発行を1カ所で行なうことを目的として、日本銀行が設立されました。④その後、一定量の銀と交換できる紙幣が発行されました（銀本位制の確立）。⑤紙幣の流通量を減らした結果、激しいデフレになり、農産物の値段が急落して、都市へ労働者として働きに出る農民が増えました。
⑥**松方デフレ**により、物価の安定と低利子率、労働者の形成がもたらされると、**企業勃興**と呼ばれる企業設立ブームが起こりました。⑦鉄道や紡績会社設立には多額の資金が必要でした。⑧その際には、銀行が設立される企業の株式を担保として、その株主に株式購入のための資金を貸し付ける「株式担保金融」というしくみも活用されました。

①The denationalized factories and mines became profitable,
民営化された 利益になる

and the political contractors, who bought the facilities from
政商 設備

the government, formed various Zaibatsu.

②After winning the Japanese-Sino war in 1897, the Japanese
日清戦争

government gained a large amount of money from
手に入れた 多額の

reparations. ③Using these funds, the Japanese government
〜を使って 資金

shifted from a silver standard to a gold standard. ④The
移行した 銀本位制 金本位制

government also utilized the funds to construct a national
使った 建設する 官営の

ironworks, "The *Yawata* Steel Works". ⑤Using subsidies
八幡製鉄所 補助金

from the government, shipping companies started to operate
操業を始めた

regular lines one after another, while domestic ship building
次々に 国内の

industries developed as well.
同様に

⑥The Zaibatsu, such as *Mitsui*, *Mitsubishi*, *Sumitomo* and

Yasuda, established organizational structures centered on a
組織形態 集中する

holding company and carried out diversified operations
持ち株会社 行なった 多角的な 経営

including finance, trade and mining. ⑦In this way, Japanese
このように

capitalism was established.
資本主義

⑧In contrast, the workers were frustrated with the bad
　　反対に　　　　　　　　　　　　　　　　不満を持った
working conditions, which caused the labor movement to
　　　　　　　　　　　　　　　　　　　労働運動
intensify.
激しくなった

70. 日本の産業革命②

①民営化された工場や鉱山はやがて黒字に転じ、払い下げを受けた政商は**財閥**を形成しました。

②1895年、日清戦争で勝利した日本は、多額の賠償金を得ました。

③その資金を使って、1897年には銀本位制から金本位制に移行しました。④また、政府はこの資金を使って、官営の製鉄所である八幡製鉄所を建設しました。⑤政府からの補助金により、海運会社は次々に定期航路を開設し、国内の造船業も発達しました。

⑥三井、三菱、住友、安田といった財閥は、持株会社を中心とする組織形態を整え、金融・貿易・鉱山業など、多角的に経営を行ないました。⑦こうして日本の資本主義が確立しました。

⑧反面、劣悪な労働条件で働く労働者は大きな不満を持つようになり、労働運動が激化するようになりました。

71. Urbanization and Electrification

①The growth rate of the Japanese economy in the 1920s after World
　　　 成長率

War 1 was relatively high on a global level. ②The factors that
　　　　　 比較的に　　　　　　　　　　　　　　　　　　　要素

supported the economy were the expansion of personal consumption,
～を支えた　　　　　　　　　　　　拡大　　　　個人消費

investment by the government sector, and capital investment in the
　　　　　　　　政府部門　　　　　　　　資本投資

private sector of power and related industries. ③With the rapid
民間部門　　　　　　　　　　　　　　　　　　　　　　　　激増

increase in labor migration from rural areas to cities, urbanization,
　　　　 労働者 移住　　　 農村　　　　　　　都市化

which is symbolized by the extension of private railways and the
　　　～に象徴される

development of residential areas in the Kansai area and Tokyo, had
開発　　　　　住宅地

progressed rapidly. ④Due to the roads, water and sewage systems,
　　　　　　　　　　　　　　　　　　上下水道

schools, parks, and other necessary facilities for the construction of a
　　　　　　　　　　　　　　　　施設　　　　建設

"city," fiscal spending of the central government and the regional
　　　 財政支出　　　　　中央の　　　　　　　　　　 地方の

governments expanded due to the movement of disarmament. ⑤In
　　　　　　 拡大した　　　　　　軍縮の動き

1914, when the Inawashiro Power Station, which had twice the
　　　　　　猪苗代発電所

power generation capacity of the conventional power station, was
発電能力　　　　　　　　　　　　従来の

completed, a boom in large-scale power development occurred.
　　　　　　ブーム　　　大規模な　電源開発

⑥As a result, electricity charges dropped. ⑦The use of electric power
　　　　　　 電気料金　　　　　　　　　　　　　　　　 電力源

source has advanced, and power consumption in the 1920s had increased
　　　 進んだ　　　　　　電力消費量

3.8 times. ⑧This was also the reason for the expansion of electric railway
　3.8倍　　　　　　　　　　　　　　　　　　〜の理由　　拡大　　　　　電鉄事業
business in large cities. ⑨In addition, the progress of the electric power
　　　　　　　　　　　　　　　　　　加えて　　　進展
industry had promoted the development of emerging industries such as the
　　　　　　促した　　　　　　　　　　　　　　　　　　　　新興産業
electrochemical industry and the electrical machinery industry. ⑩Thus, the
電気化学工業　　　　　　　　　　　　電気機械産業　　　　　　　　　　　こうして
era of full-scale heavy chemical industrialization came to Japan.
時代　　本格的な　　重化学工業

71. 都市化と電化

①第1次世界大戦後1920年代における日本経済の成長率は、世界水準からすると相対的に高水準にありました。②景気を下支えしたのは、個人消費の拡大と政府部門の投資、そして民間部門の電力業およびその関連産業の設備投資でした。③農村から都市への労働移動が激増すると、関西圏や東京における私鉄の延伸と住宅地の開発に象徴される都市化が急速に進みました。④「都市」建設に必要な道路や上下水道、学校、公園などの整備のため、中央・地方の財政支出は軍縮の流れも相まって拡大しました。⑤1914年に従来の2倍の発電能力をもつ猪苗代発電所が完成すると、大規模電源開発のブームが起こりました。⑥それにより、電力料金は低下しました。⑦電気の動力源としての利用が進み、1920年代の電力消費量は3.8倍に伸びました。⑧大都市での電鉄事業拡大もこうした背景によるものです。⑨また、電力業の進展は、電気化学工業や、電気機械工業といった新興産業の発展を促しました。⑩こうして日本にも本格的な重化学工業化の時代が訪れるのです。

72. The Showa Depression

①The *Showa* Depression was a deep economic downturn
昭和恐慌   景気の低迷

which lasted from 1930 to 1931. ②During World War 1, which

began in 1914, the Japanese economy blossomed because
                                                                              発展した

military equipment was ordered by the U.S. and European
軍需物資

countries. ③However, after the war, the economy slowed down
                                                                                          減速した

and Japan was devastated by the Great *Kanto* earthquake. ④In
      ～で壊滅的な被害を受けた 関東大震災

1927, as the earthquake restoration bonds became bad debts, a
                                            復興   不良債権

slip of tongue by the Minister of Finance set off a financial
                                                          引き起こした 金融恐慌

recession, and as a result, many banks and companies went
                                                                                        倒産した

bankrupt. ⑤Two years later, in 1929, the stock prices collapsed
                                                              株価   暴落した

in the New York Stock Market, which brought the world to

the Great Depression. ⑥In 1930, the *Hamaguchi* Cabinet
世界恐慌   内閣

adopted two economic policies, fiscal austerity and a reversion
実施した   緊縮財政   復帰

to the gold standard, which led to a higher yen rate and to the
          金本位制   減少

decline in exports. ⑦With the decline in consumption,
                                      ～にともない   消費

numerous companies went bankrupt and many people lost
非常に多くの～

their jobs. ⑧It was *Takahashi Korekiyo*, a Minister of Finance
                        大蔵大臣

of the *Inukai* Cabinet, who ended the *Showa* Depression. [9] He

banned the gold standard and this led to a lower yen rate, which
停止した　金本位制　　　　　　　　　　　　　　導く

increased exports. [10] And he was able to raise the productivity by
　　　　　　　　　　　　　　　　　　高める　生産力

issuing government bonds and increasing public investments. [11]
発行すること　国債　　　　　　　　　　　　　公共投資

His policies are well known because they were successful and

preceded Keynes' theories (see p.86).
先行して　　ケインズ理論

72. 昭和恐慌

①**昭和恐慌**とは、1930 〜 1931 年にかけて起きた恐慌です。②1914年に始まった第1次世界大戦では、欧米から軍需物資などの受注があり、日本は好景気になりました。③しかし、戦後は景気が減速し、1923 年に起こった関東大震災では壊滅的な被害を受けました。④1927 年、震災復興のために発行した手形が不良債権化するなか、当時の大蔵大臣の失言がきっかけとなって**金融恐慌**が起こり、銀行や企業が相次いで倒産しました。⑤2 年後の 1929 年に、ニューヨーク証券取引所の株価が大暴落し「**世界恐慌**」に突入しました。⑥1930年に浜口内閣は、緊縮財政と金解禁（金本位制への復帰）という経済政策を実施しましたが、円高に傾き、輸出が不振になりました。⑦消費が落ち込み、多くの企業が倒産し、大量の失業者を出しました。⑧この昭和恐慌を終息させたのが、犬養内閣の蔵相・高橋是清でした。⑨金解禁をやめ、円安に誘導して輸出額を増加させました。⑩また、国債を発行、公共投資をして国民の生産力を上げました。⑪高橋是清の政策はケインズ理論（p.86 参照）よりも先行していたことで有名です。

73. The Economic Blocs and the Entry into the War

①The great western powers made economic blocs composed
of their own countries and their colonies, and protected them
with a high tariff barrier in order to recover from the
economic damages which they received during the Great
Depression of 1929. ②Although Japanese exports had been
strong, trade decreased because of the difficulty in exporting
commodities to the various blocs.

③After the Japanese-Sino war, the Japanese-Russo war and
World War 1, Japan engineered the Manchurian Incident and
established the State of Manchuria in northeast China in 1931.
④Subsequently, Japan sent many farmers who had suffered
from the *Showa* Depression as armed settlers to *Manchukuo*.
⑤Japan tried to create a bloc which included Taiwan, the Korean
Peninsula and *Manchukuo* to be competitive with the blocs of
the great western powers. ⑥This led Japan into the way of fascism.
⑦In 1939, when World War 2 broke out, the Japanese army
invaded south-eastern Asia for resources; which plunged

Japan into the Pacific War in 1941. ⑧The Japanese economic
太平洋戦争

system shifted from a free economy to a controlled economy
統制された

under the "National General Mobilization Act". ⑨The
国家総動員法

government issued a huge number of government bonds to
大量の　　　　　　　　　国債

cover the expense of military costs, which caused runaway
補う　　費用　　　　　　　　　　　　　　　　　　　　激しい

inflation after World War 2.

73. ブロック経済と参戦

①1929 年に発生した世界恐慌から経済を立て直すために、欧
米列強は、自国と植民地をブロック（塊）として保護し、他の
ブロックには高い関税障壁を設ける、ブロック経済の体制をと
りました。②輸出が好調な日本でしたが、ブロックへの輸出が
困難になり、貿易額が減少しました。

③日清戦争、日露戦争、第 1 次世界大戦を経た日本は、1931 年
に満州事変を起こし、満州国(中国の東北部)を建国しました。④昭
和恐慌で苦しんでいた多くの農民を武装させ、満州国に移民とし
て送りました。⑤当時、植民地化していた台湾と朝鮮に満州を加
えたブロックを構築し、欧米列強のブロックに対抗しようとした
のです。⑥こうして日本はファシズムに向かい進んでいきます。

⑦1939 年に第 2 次世界大戦が勃発すると、日本陸軍は南方（東
南アジア）に資源を求めて侵攻し、1941 年に太平洋戦争に突
入します。⑧日本の経済体制は、自由経済から「国家総動員法」
下の戦時統制経済に変わりました。⑨軍需などのために国債が
大量に発行され、戦後の激しいインフレの原因になりました。

74. Democratization of the Economy

①After the war ended, under the control of the General
　　　　　　　　　　　　　　　　　　　　　総司令部
Headquarters of the Allied Force (GHQ), Japan abolished
　　　　　　　　　連合国軍　　　　　　　　　　　　　廃止した
militarism and pursued democratizing the economy with three
軍国主義　　　進めた　　民主化すること
agendas; the dismantling of the Zaibatsu (financial groups), the
計画　　　解体
farmland reform and the creation of three labor laws.
農地改革　　　　　　　　制定　　　　　　労働法
②The government dismantled the Zaibatsu, which had
　　　　　　　　　解体した
functioned as the financial base of the militarism, and exiled
機能してきた　　　　　　　　　　　　　　　　　　　追放した
their executive officers and their families from the economic
　　幹部職　　　　　　　　　　　　　　　　　　経済界
community. ③However, the dismantlement was less than
　　　　　　　　　　　　　解体　　　　　　　決して～ではない
perfect because companies that had belonged to each Zaibatsu
完全な
had created cross-shareholding groups (see p.76) after April
　　　　　　　株式持ち合い
1952, at the end of the occupation. ④The farmland reform
　　　　　　　　　　占領期間
abolished the parasitic landlord system. ⑤This was the Japanese
　　　　　寄生地主制度
agricultural system before World War 2, in which a landlord
農業の
rents land to the tenant farmers and imposes a high rate of
～に土地を貸す　小作人　　　　　　　課す
rent on them. ⑥The government bought land where landlords
地代
were not living or which exceeded a certain area size, and sold it
　　　　　　　　　　　　　　　　ある一定の　面積

to tenant farmers for a low price. ⑦In 1949, about 87% of the
<u>およそ</u>

farmers became <u>owner farmers</u>, which <u>motivated</u> the farmers
　　　　　　　自作農　　　　　　　　　　　　　やる気が上がった

and <u>heightened</u> their <u>productivity</u>. ⑧<u>Additionally</u>, the <u>Labor</u>
　　　向上した　　　　　　生産性　　　　　　加えて　　　　　　　労働組合法

<u>Union Act</u>, the <u>Labor Standard Act</u> and the <u>Labor</u>
　　　　　　　　　　　　　労働基準法　　　　　　　　　　労働関係調整法

<u>Relations Adjustment Act</u> were established which protected

workers' <u>rights</u> and <u>consequently</u> increased their voice.
　　　　　権利　　　　　その結果

74. 経済の民主化

①敗戦後の日本は、GHQ（連合国総司令部）の指導のもと、軍国主義と経済統制を廃止し、「**財閥の解体**」、「**農地改革**」、「**労働法制定**」の３つの経済の民主化が進められました。

②「軍国主義の経済的基盤」として機能した財閥を解体し、その幹部と家族を経済界から追放しました。③しかし、1952年4月に占領期間が終了すると、財閥系の企業が株式持ち合い（p.76参照）でグループを作るなど、財閥の完全な解体とはいえませんでした。④「農地改革」とは、寄生地主制度の廃止です。⑤戦前は地主が小作人と呼ばれる農民に土地を貸し、高額な小作料を物納させる制度がありました。⑥地主が不在で貸し付けている土地や一定の広さを超えた土地は政府が買い取り、安価で小作人に売却しました。⑦1949年には農民のおよそ87%が自作農となり、意欲が高まって生産性が向上しました。

⑧また、「労働組合法」、「労働基準法」、「労働関係調整法」が定められたことにより、労働者の権利を認められ、発言力が高まりました。

75. The Dodge Line

①In 1946, the *Yoshida Shigeru* Cabinet, first of all, concentrated investments in the coal industry as an energy resource and the steel industry as the support for various industries, in order to raise depressed production. ②The Reconstruction Finance Bank (RFB) was established in order to lend funds necessary for economic recovery. ③Since the bank issued a volume of bonds and the Bank of Japan underwrote them, money started to circulate. ④This would later became a factor in the currency expansion which caused the "RFB inflation".

⑤When the Cold War escalated between the U.S. and USSR[*], the U.S. shifted the occupational policy from the "demilitarization of Japan" to the "stabilization of the Japanese economy". ⑥The U.S. intent was for Japan to be a "safeguard against Communism". ⑦In 1948, the General Headquarters of the Allied Force invited an American banker, Joseph Dodge, and instituted the "Nine Doctrines for Economic Security" to

[*] USSR：Union of Soviet Socialist Republics

force Japan to make a drastic economic change (the Dodge
　　　　　　　　　～が—することを推し進める　　　　思い切った

Line). ⑧The three major policies were as follows: balancing the
　　　　　　　　　　　　　　　　　　　　　　　　　　収支を合わせる

budget, dissolving of the RFB and establishing a fixed
予算　　　　解散(→廃止)　　　　　　　　　　制定　　　　　　固定為替相場

exchange rate of 360 yen to 1 U.S. dollar. ⑨As a result, the
　　　　　　　　　　　　　　～につき　　　　　　その結果

inflation was reduced and the revenue of the budget exceeded
　　　　　収まった　　　　　　　歳入　　　　　　　　　　上回った

the expenditures.
歳出

75. ドッジ・ライン

①1946年、吉田茂内閣は、落ち込んだ生産を上げるために、ま
ずエネルギー源としての石炭産業と、さまざまな産業の基盤とな
る鉄鋼産業に集中的に資金を投入しました。②経済復興に必要な
資金を貸し付けるために、復興金融金庫（復金）がつくられまし
た。③復金債という公債が大量に発行され、これを日銀が引き受
けたため、世の中にお金が出回りました。④これが通貨膨張の要
因にもなり、復金インフレを招きました。
⑤米国とソ連の冷戦が激化すると、米国は占領政策の基本方針を
「日本の非軍事化」から「日本経済の安定化」に変えました。⑥こ
れには、日本を「反共の防波堤」とする目的がありました。⑦1948
年にGHQは経済安定9原則を設け、米国から銀行家のドッジを
呼び、厳しい改革（ドッジ・ライン）を実施させました。⑧内容
は、「均衡予算（歳入に見合った歳出となる予算）をたてること」、
「復興金融金庫の廃止」、「1ドル＝360円の固定為替相場の設定」
などです。⑨その結果、インフレは収まり、歳入が歳出を上回り
ました。

76. The High Economic Growth

①When the Korean War broke out in 1950, the Japanese
  朝鮮戦争   勃発した
economy bloomed because food and military equipment were
        栄えた   軍需工業
ordered by the U.S. military which fought for the South
受注された   ～と戦う   韓国
Koreans, this in turn increased the demand. ②The textile
            次々に 増加した   需要   繊維
industry and the metal industry grew significantly. ③Mineral
              金属   著しく   鉱工業製品
or industrial products were able to recover to levels before the
                                回復する
war. ④The government focused on heavy industries such as
                    ～に力を入れた 重工業
electric power, shipbuilding and steel industries, so that the
電力   造船   鉄鋼
rate of manufacturers, represented by heavy industries,
比率   製造業   ～に代表される   重工業
increased in the industrial structure. ⑤Oil started to be used
              産業構造
as an energy resource instead of coal.
                    ～の代わりに

⑥From 1955, 10 years after the end of World War 2, for 18

years, Japan experienced a high economic development in
            経験した   発展
which the growth rate was over 10%. ⑦The causes of this
        成長率   原因
growth are as follows: there were many low-wage laborers
        次のように   低賃金の 労働者
from farm villages and local areas; people saved their money
      農村   地方
to a great extent and the money was used for business
  かなり多く

investments; the exchange rate, fixed at 360 yen to one U.S.
為替レート

dollar, was favorable to export goods; and companies
有利で

made efforts to introduce innovations from Europe and
〜することに努力した　　　　　　技術

the U.S., and to improve on them. ⑧Japan made an
改良する

astonishing recovery from the devastation of World War 2
驚異的な　　　　　　　　　　荒廃

and achieved a miraculous economic growth.
なし遂げた　　奇跡的な

76. 高度経済成長

①1950年に始まった朝鮮戦争で、韓国側についた米国の軍需物資や食料の受注があり、日本は好景気を迎えます(特需景気)。②繊維産業や金属産業が大いに発展しました※。③鉱工業の生産高も戦前のレベルにまで復活しました。④政府は電力、造船、鉄鋼などの重工業に力を入れ、産業構造においても重工業に代表される製造業の比率が伸びました。⑤エネルギー源は石炭から石油に転換しました。

⑥敗戦から10年たった1955年から、18年間にわたり、経済成長率が平均10%を超える**高度経済成長**が続きました。⑦この成長の要因としては、「農村や地方から出稼ぎに行く賃金の安い労働者がたくさんいた」、「国民がよく貯蓄をし、そのお金が企業の設備投資にあてられた」、「円のレートが360円とUSドルに対して安く固定されていたので、輸出に有利であった」、「欧米の技術革新を導入し、改善する努力をした」ことなどが挙げられます。⑧戦後の日本は驚異的な復興をし、奇跡的な成長を遂げたのです。

※ 繊維の文字から「糸へん景気」、金属の文字から「金へん景気」といわれた。

77. The Oil Shock

①In 1973, crude oil prices rose sharply and the oil shock hit the
　　　　　　 原油　　　　　　　　　　　 激しく　　　　　　 オイルショック
world. ②During the period of high economic growth, Japan had
　　　　　　　　　　　　　　　　 高度経済成長
imported cheap crude oil from the Middle East. ③In the Middle
　　　　　　　　　　　　　　　　　　　 中東
East, the Palestinian issue had been a conflict between
　　　 パレスチナ問題　　　　　　　　　　　　 紛争
Israel and the Arab countries. ④When the Fourth Middle East
　　　　　　　　　　　　　　　　　　　　 第4次中東戦争
War broke out in 1973, the Arab countries reduced crude oil
　　 勃発した　　　　　　　　　　　　　　　　 減らした
exports to the U.S., Europe and Japan which were friendly to
輸出
Israel. ⑤Resultant to this, the Organization of Petroleum
　　　　 この結果として　　　　 OPEC（石油輸出国機構）
Exporting Countries (OPEC) raised the price of crude oil to
　　　　　　　　　　　　　　 引き上げた
4 times more than before, and the oil shock hit the world.
　4倍
⑥Increasing the oil price had a big impact on the Japanese
　～が高騰すること　　　　　　　　　 影響
economy, and the economic growth rate fell below zero for
　　　　　　　 経済成長率　　　　　　　　 ゼロ以下に
the first time after World War 2. ⑦People experienced panic
初めて　　　　　　　　　　　　　　 経験した
as rumors were spreading, for example "toilet paper would be
　　 噂
sold out because the oil price was too high". ⑧Following the
　　　　　　　　　　　　　　　　　　　　　 ～を受けて
oil shock, the stagflation continued in which the economic
　　　　 スタグフレーション
growth rate slowed down while the inflation rate remained
　　　　　　　　　　　 一方　　　　　　　　　　　　 ～のままである

182

high. ⑨In Japan, since each company improved business
　　　　　　　　　　　　　　　　　　向上させた　　経営効率化
efficiency and effective resource utilization, inflation slowed
　　　　　　効果的な　資源活用　　　　　　　　　　　　　落ち着いた
down earlier than other countries. ⑩Owing to the oil shock
　　　　　　　　　　　　　　　　　　　　　　　　　～のおかげで
and the Nixon shock (see p.144) which occurred 2 years prior
　　　ニクソン・ショック　　　　　　　　　　　起きた　　　　　前に
to the oil shock, the high economic growth ended and Japan

moved into an era of stable economic growth.
　　　　　　　　時代(期)　安定

77. オイルショック

①1973年に石油価格が暴騰し、**オイルショック**が起きました。②高
度経済成長期に、日本は中東から安価な石油を大量に輸入してい
ました。③中東では、アラブ各国とイスラエルの「**パレスチナ問題**」
がありました。④1973年に始まった第4次中東戦争で、アラブ各
国は、イスラエルに好意的な欧米や日本に対して、石油の輸出を
制限しました。⑤それを受け、OPEC（石油輸出国機構）が原油価
格を4倍に引き上げ、世界中でオイルショックが起きました。
⑥日本経済は大打撃を受け、1974年に戦後初めて経済成長率が
マイナスになりました。⑦原油高騰でトイレットペーパーが品不
足になるという噂が広まり、一時パニックになりました※。⑧オ
イルショックの後、経済成長率が下がっているのにインフレ率が
高い状況（スタグフレーション）が続きました。⑨日本では、各
企業が経営の効率化をはかり省資源化を実行したので、他国に比
べ、早期にインフレが収束しました。⑩オイルショックとその2
年前に起きたニクソン・ショック（p.144参照）で、日本の高度
経済成長期は終わりを告げ、安定成長期に移行しました。

※ 原油価格が70%上がり、石油関連商品に限らず、あらゆる商品の価格が高騰すると
　噂され、買占めが起こった。マスコミによる報道も人々のパニックを加速させた。

78. The Bubble Economy

①The yen exchange rate rose rapidly during a period of 3
上がった

years from around 240 yen to around 120 yen per 1 dollar in

1988 because of the Plaza Accord in 1985 (see p.148).
〜により   プラザ合意

②Exports decreased and the Japanese economy entered into
輸出   減少した   〜に突入した

a high yen recession. ③The Bank of Japan decreased the
円高不況   日本銀行

official discount rate gradually from 5% to 2.5% which was
公定歩合   徐々に

the lowest rate at that time, so that companies could easily
                          〜するように

borrow money from banks. ④However, large companies
借りる   大企業

borrowed money from abroad because of financial and capital
海外   金融・資本市場

market liberalization. ⑤They managed funds using the money
自由化   運用した

borrowing from abroad, in commodities such as stocks.
株

⑥As a result of the decreasing number of loans to large
〜の結果   〜の減少   融資

companies, the bank shifted loans to small-to-midsize
移った   中小企業

companies of sectors such as construction, real-estate and
部門   建設会社   不動産

nonbanking. ⑦As companies and investors, funded by loans
ノンバンク   融資を受けた

from banks, invested in real-estate, the prices increased greatly.
投資した

⑧Since investors were reinvesting funds earned from their prior
投資家   〜を一に再投資した   前の

investments, into stocks and real estate, prices continued to rise.

⑨At the end of 1989, the Nikkei index recorded 38,915
　　　　　　　　　　　　日経平均株価指数
yen, the highest rate in its history. ⑩This phenomenon in
　　　　　　　　　　　　　　　　　　　現象
which real estate and stock prices rise much higher than their

intrinsic worth is the "bubble economy". ⑪During the bubble
本来の　　価値　　　　　　　バブル経済
period, demands increased and the economy blossomed.

78. バブル景気

①1985年の「プラザ合意」（p.148参照）により、3年後の1988年には1ドル240円前後から、120円前後へと、急激な円高になりました。②日本は輸出不振に陥り、円高不況が発生しました。③日銀は5%だった公定歩合を、段階的に当時の最低水準の2.5%まで引き下げ、企業が銀行から資金を借りやすい状態にしました。④しかし、金融・資本市場の自由化により、大企業は海外から資金を調達するようになりました。⑤大企業は海外から得た資金で、株式投資などを運用しました。

⑥大企業への融資が減った銀行は、貸付先を中小の建設会社、不動産、ノンバンク※などの部門へ移しました。⑦融資を得た会社や投資家が不動産に投資したので、地価が大幅に上昇しました。⑧投資家は、増えた資金を株や土地に再投資し、価格は上昇し続けました。⑨1989年末の日経平均株価は、3万8915円という史上最高値を記録しました。⑩このように、株価や地価が本来の価値よりも大きく膨れ上がる現象がバブルです。⑪バブル期には需要が増え、大変な好景気になりました。

※ ノンバンクとは、預金等を扱わず、融資のみを行なう金融機関。信販会社、リース会社、クレジット会社など。

79. The Collapse of Bubble Economy

①During the bubble period, many people and companies
バブル時代

invested their real estate or financial assets to earn through
運用した   土地   金融資産   ～を稼ぐ

capital gain, which was called the "financial management
資産売却益(キャピタル・ゲイン)   財テク

technique". ②As many of them began to invest abroad, the
海外に

monetary economy expanded.
マネー経済   拡大した

③In order to cool the overheated bubble economy, the Bank
抑える   過熱した   日本銀行

of Japan adopted a tight money policy in 1989 and,
採用した   金融引き締め政策

after that, it began gradually increasing the official discount
徐々に   公定歩合

rate . ④The official discount rate was increased to 6%, and

the lending interest rate of banks increased accordingly.
融資の金利   それに応じて

⑤The government also adopted a policy to control land
規制する

transactions as follows: to control the total volume and the
土地の取引   総量

financing arrangements for loans to purchase real estate, to
資金調達   融資   購入する

introduce land price taxes, and to increase real estate taxes.
導入する   地価税   固定資産税

⑥As a result of the policies of the government and the BOJ,
～の結果

the stock prices collapsed in 1990 after stock prices recorded
株価   暴落した   記録した

the highest rate ever. ⑦Next, land prices started to fall, and
これまでに

therefore the bubble collapsed at the beginning of 1991.
そのために　　　　　　　　はじけた

⑧The companies, which had borrowed money from banks on

the collateral of real estate, could not repay the debts, because
担保　　　　　　　　　　　　　　　　返す　　　借金

land prices fell. ⑨Consequently, banks held a large amount
その結果　　　　　　　　　大量の

of bad loans which would never be repaid.
不良債権　　　　　　　　　　　　返済される

79. バブル崩壊

①バブル期には、たくさんの人々や会社が、所有する土地や金融資産を運用してキャピタル・ゲインを得る「財テク」を行ないました。②その多くが海外投資を行なったことで、マネー経済が拡大しました。③その過熱したバブル経済に対し、日銀が1989年から公定歩合を段階的に引き上げる金融引き締め政策を始めました。④最終的には1990年に6%まで引き上げ、金融機関は融資の金利を上げました。⑤政府も1990年から、「金融機関に対して総量規制をし、土地関連の融資を抑制」、「地価税を導入」、「固定資産税を増額」などの政策を出し、土地取引に関する規制を強めました。⑥株価が上昇のピークを迎えていたところに、日銀と政府の政策がきっかけになって、1990年に株価が暴落しました。⑦続いて地価も下がりだし、1991年の初め頃にバブルがはじけました。⑧土地を担保に、その土地の値上がりを前提に融資を受けていた企業は、地価が下がったため、借金を返すことができなくなりました。⑨その結果、銀行は大量の回収できる見込みのない債権（**不良債権**）を抱えることになりました。

80. The Financial Crisis

①In 1997, the *Hashimoto* Cabinet introduced the reform of
内閣　　　　導入した　　　改革

the fiscal structure as follows: government spending cuts,
財政構造　　　　以下のように　　　　　　　　支出

consumption tax rate increments, termination of income and
消費税率　　　　　　　増加(→引き上げ)　停止(→打ち切り)　所得

resident tax reductions, and increase of health insurance
住民　　減税　　　　　　　　　　　　健康保険

premiums. ②However, the reform was ineffective and the
保険料　　　　　　　　　　　　　　　効果がなかった

economy showed a trend towards deflation (see p.32).
傾向　　　　　　　デフレーション

③From 1997 to 1998, some financial institutions, which were
金融機関　　　　　　〜を抱えていた

burdened by bad loans, went bankrupt. ④To prevent further
不良債権　　　倒産した　　　防ぐ　　　さらなる

deterioration of business conditions, some banks were
悪化

unwilling to extend new loans, which was called a "credit
〜を嫌がって　広げる　　　　　　　　　　　　　貸し渋り

crunch", or forced to withdraw loan credit, which was called
強制する　　回収する

a "credit withdrawal". ⑤Consequently, companies went
貸しはがし　　　　　そのため

bankrupt because they had funding difficulties.

⑥In 1998, the *Obuchi* Cabinet injected public money into
投入した　公的資金

banks in order to defuse the financial crisis. ⑦A total of
打開する　金融危機

around 12.4 trillion yen had been injected by 2003.

⑧However, the effects did not appear for a long period, and the
効果　　　　　　　　　　　　長い期間

bad loans held by all the Japanese banks increased to 43 trillion
兆
yen in all.

⑨In 2002, the *Koizumi* Cabinet created a "financial

revitalization program" and helped write off bad loans. ⑩As a
再生　　　　　　　　　　　　　　　～するのを手助けする　精算する
result, the debt decreased to about 16 trillion yen by 2005.

80. 金融危機

①1997年、橋本内閣は支出の削減、消費税率の引き上げ、所得税・住民税の特別減税打ち切り、健康保険の負担増加などの財政構造改革を行ないました。②ところが、これらは功を奏さず、社会はデフレ（p.32参照）に傾きました。

③1997～98年にかけて、不良債権を抱えた金融機関のなかには破綻するところも出ました。④経営状態がより悪化するのを恐れて、企業に新規や追加の融資を控える「貸し渋り」や、今ある融資を強制的に回収する「貸しはがし」を行なう銀行もありました。⑤そのため、資金繰りの悪化した企業が多く倒産しました。

⑥1998年、小渕内閣はこのような金融危機を打破するため、公的資金を金融機関に投入しました。⑦2003年までに総額で約12兆4,000億円の公的資金が注入されました。⑧その効果は長い間現われず、全国の銀行が抱えていた不良債権は2002年に約43兆円に達しました。⑨2002年、小泉内閣では「金融再生プログラム」を設け、不良債権の処理を進めました。⑩その結果、2005年には約16兆円まで減らすことができました。

81. The "Lost" Thirty Years

①From 1991 after the collapse of the bubble economy, the
　　　　　　　　　崩壊　　　　　　　バブル経済

economic downturn continued for about twenty years and was
　　　　低迷

said to be the "lost 20 years." ②During this period, Japan
　　　　　失われた20年

could not escape from deflation, the appreciation of the yen,
　　　　　脱する　　　デフレ　　　（円の上昇）→円高

and the slump in stock prices, and consequently, the gap between
　　　低迷　　　株価

rich and poor widened. ③In March 2011, when the manufacturing
　　　　　　　　　　　　　　　　　　　　　　製造業

industry continued to slump and exports dropped, the Great East
　　　　　　　　　　　　　　　　　輸出　　落ち込んだ

Japan Earthquake struck, further damaging the economy.
　　　　　　　　　　襲った　　さらなる　打撃

④Prime Minister *Abe*, who was reappointed in December 2012,
　　首相　　　　　　　　　　　　再任した

aimed to break away from deflation and expand wealth with
ねらった　抜け出す　　　　　　　　　　　拡大する

"Abenomics" policy (See p.106). ⑤After that, the economic
　　　　　　　　　　　　　　　　　　　　　　　　経済効果

effect for the Tokyo Olympic Games was boosted, and the
　　　　　　　　　　　　　　　　　　　後押しした

economy recovered temporarily. ⑥However, wages did not rise
　　　　回復した　一時的に　　　　　　　　　賃金

so much, and many people did not feel the economic recovery.
　　　　　　　　　　　　　　　　　　　　景気回復

⑦Due to the spread of the new coronavirus infection in
　　　　拡大　　　　　新型コロナウィルス感染

China in December 2019, entry from overseas was restricted
　　　　　　　　　　　　　　　　　　　　　制限された

and the Tokyo Olympic Games were postponed. ⑧As a result,
　　　　　　　　　　　　　　　　延期になった　　その結果

many industries were hit, including the tourism industry, which
打撃を受けた
relied on inbound tourism, and the restaurant business, which
〜に頼った　インバウンド観光
was requested to self-regulate. [9]The situation of economic
要求された　　　　　　　自粛する　　　　　　　　　　　経済の停滞
stagnation that has continued to experience intermittent deflation
断続的なデフレ
from the early 1990s to the present is sometimes called
1990年代前半から現在まで
the "lost thirty years".

81. 失われた 30 年

①バブル崩壊後の 1991 年から約 20 年間は、経済の低迷が続き「失われた 20 年」と言われました。②この間、日本はデフレと円高、株価の低迷から脱することができず、貧富の格差が広がりました。③製造業の不振が続き、輸出が落ち込んだ 2011 年 3 月、東日本大震災が発生し、経済はさらなる打撃を受けました。④2012 年 12 月に再任した安倍首相は、「アベノミクス」で、デフレ脱却と富の拡大を狙いました（P.106 参照）。⑤その後、東京オリンピック大会に向けた経済効果も後押しし、景気は一時回復しました。⑥しかし賃金はあまり上がらず、多くの国民は景気回復の実感を得られませんでした。⑦2019 年 12 月、中国で発生した新型コロナウィルス感染拡大で、海外からの入国が制限され、東京オリンピックも延期になりました。⑧その結果、インバウンドに頼っていた観光業や営業自粛の飲食業などを始め、多くの産業が打撃を受けました。⑨このような、1990 年代前半から現在まで断続的にデフレが続く経済低迷の状況は、「失われた 30 年」と呼ばれることもあります。

82. Innovations that Support the Future Japanese Economy

①The remarkable progress in information and communication
目覚ましい　　　進歩　　　　情報通信技術

technology is about to change people's lives. ②This big change is
～しようとしている　　　　　暮らし

called the 4th Industrial Revolution , and IoT, AI, and big data
第4次産業革命

are the three pillars that support this. ③By combining these, it
柱　　　　支える　　　　　組み合わせること

becomes possible to share vast amounts of knowledge and
膨大な量

information, and control machines and robots. ④For example, in a
制御する

self-driving car, it will be possible to determine the route from
自動運転車　　　　　　　　　　　　　　決定する　　　　経路

various information such as weather, past traffic volume, and
過去の交通量

events taking place in the surrounding area. ⑤These technologies
～で行われる　　　周囲地域

reduce the burden on the person required to collect and analyze
負担を減らす

necessary information, and also remove restrictions on work and
取り除く　制約

range of action due to age and disabilities.
行動範囲　　　　　　　　障害

⑥The government has proposed Society 5.0 as a future
提唱している

image of Japanese society that utilizes these. ⑦Society 5.0 is
活用する

defined as "a human-centered society that achieves both
定義されている　　人間中心の社会　　　　　　　実現する

economic development and the solution of social issues
解決

through a system that highly integrates real space and virtual
高度に融合する　　　現実空間　　　　　仮想空間

space". ⑧If this is realized, it will open the way to

overcoming issues such as the declining birthrate and aging
　　　　　克服すること　　　　　　　　　　　　少子高齢化
population, depopulation of rural areas, and the gap
　　　　　　　　過疎化　　　　　地方　　　　　　　　貧富の格差
between rich and poor. ⑨Beyond that, new added value will
　　　　　　　　　　　　　　　　それを超えて　　　　付加価値
be created, and the economy must revitalized.
　　　　　　　　　　　　　　再び活性化する

82. 未来の日本経済を支えるイノベーション

①情報通信技術の目覚ましい進歩は、人々の暮らしまで大きく変えようとしています。②この大きな変化は**第4次産業革命**と呼ばれ、**IoT、AI、ビッグデータ**がこれを支える3本柱です。③これらが組み合わさることで、膨大な知識や情報を共有して、機械やロボットを制御することが可能になります。④たとえばクルマの自動運転では、天候や過去の交通量、周囲で行われるイベントなど、様々な情報から経路を決定することができるようになります。⑤こうした技術は、必要な情報の収集や分析に要する人の負担を軽減し、年齢や障害等による労働や行動範囲の制約も取り払います。

⑥政府はこれらを活用した日本社会の将来の姿として、Society 5.0 を提唱しています。⑦Society 5.0 は「現実空間と仮想空間を高度に融合させたシステムにより、経済発展と社会的課題の解決を両立する、人間中心の社会」と定義されています。⑧これが実現すれば、少子高齢化や地方の過疎化、貧富の格差などの課題克服にも道が開けます。⑨その先には新しい付加価値も生まれ、経済は再び活性化するに違いありません。

本書に関連した略年表
Short Chronology

World events / 世界の出来事 　 Japanese events / 日本の出来事

	年号	出来事	参照ページ
江戸時代 Edo period	1760年代	イギリスで産業革命が始まる。 The industrial revolution starts In England.	p46
	1776年	アダム・スミスの『国富論』が出版される。 "Wealth of Nations" by Adam Smith is published.	p18 p46
	1867年	マルクスの『資本論』が出版される。 "The Capital Volume One" by Marx is published.	p70
	1867年	新政府による国家体制が築かれる。 The New Government builds a national system.	p164
明治時代 Meiji period（1868〜1912年）	1869年	戊辰戦争が終結する。 The Boshin War ends.	p164
	1870年頃	明治政府が「殖産興業」、「富国強兵」を推進する。 The Meiji government puts into action "the encouragement of new industry" policy and "increasing wealth and military power" policy.	p164
	1872年	『鉱山心得』が発令され、すべての鉱物は政府に属するとされる。 "The rule of mine" is announced. All mineral rights are declared government property.	—
	1872年	官営模範工場の1つである富岡製糸場が開業する。 Tomioka silk-mill, one of the government-run model factories, starts operating.	—
	1873年	地租改正が行なわれる。 "Land tax reforms" are implemented.	p164
	1873年頃〜	三井、三菱などの政商が、政府の殖産興業政策と結びついた利権を持つ。 Some private entrepreneurs such as Mitsui and Mitsubishi, known as "political contractors" made alliances with the government under "the encouragement of new industry" policy.	p164
	1876年頃	不換紙幣が発行される。 Fiat money is issued .	p164
	1877年	西南戦争が終結する。 The Seinan War ends.	p164
	1880年	官営の工業や鉱山の払い下げが始まり、政商が財閥を形成するようになる。 The government sells national factories and mines to political contractors who form Zaibatsu.	p168
	1881年	松方デフレ政策が行なわれる。 "Matsukata Deflation" policy is adopted.	p166
	1882年	日本銀行が設立される。 The Bank of Japan is established.	p166
	1882年	銀本位制が導入される。 The silver standard is adopted.	p166
	1880年代後半	企業設立が相次ぐ。（企業勃興） A boom to establish companies occurs (the increase of business enterprises).	p166
	1893年	三菱合資会社が設立される。 Mitsubishi limited partnership company is established.	—
	1895年	日清戦争が終結する。 The Japanese-Sino war ends.	p168
	1897年	金本位制が導入される。 A gold standard is adopted.	p168

	1897年	日本初の労働組合が結成される。 Japan's first labor union is formed.	—
	1901年	八幡製鉄所が操業を開始する。 "The Yawata Steel Works" starts operating.	p168
	1905年	日露戦争が終結する。 The Japanese-Russo war ends.	—
	1909年	三井財閥、三井合名会社を頂点とするコンツェルン体制が確立する。 Mitsui zaibatsu is established modelled on the Konzern structure with the Mitsui general partnership company at the top.	—
大正時代 Taishō period	1914年	第1次世界大戦が勃発する。 World War I breaks out.	p172
	1918年	第1次世界大戦が終結する。 World War 1 ends.	p174
	1920年	戦後恐慌が起こる。 Postwar recession occurs in Japan.	p172
	1923年	関東大震災が起こる。 The Great Kanto Earthquake occurs.	p172
昭和時代 Shōwa period（1926〜1989年）	1927年	金融恐慌が起こる。 A financial recession develops.	p172
	1929年	世界恐慌が起こる。 The Great Depression begins.	p172
	1930年	昭和恐慌が起こる。 The Showa Depression occurs.	p172
	1931年	金本位制へ復帰する。 The gold standard is readopted.	p172
	1931年	高橋是清大蔵大臣が金輸出を再禁止し、新たな経済政策を始める。 Korekiyo Takahashi, Minister of Finance rebans gold exports and launches new economic policy.	p172
	1931年	満州事変が勃発する。 The Manchurian Incident is engineered.	p174
	1933年	米国でニューディール政策が行なわれる。 The New Deal program is implemented in the U.S.	p86
	1936年	ケインズの『雇用・利子および貨幣の一般理論』が出版される。 "The General Theory of Employment, Interest and Money" by Keynes is published.	p86
	1938年	国家総動員法が出される。 The "National General Mobilization Act" is announced.	p174
	1939年	第2次世界大戦が勃発する。 World War 2 breaks out.	p174
	1941年	太平洋戦争が勃発する。 The Pacific War breaks out.	p174
	1944年	ブレトン・ウッズ会議が開かれる。 The Bretton Woods agreement is concluded.	p140
	1945年	ヤルタ会談が開かれ、冷戦が始まる。 The Cold War starts at the Yalta Conference.	—
	1945年	第2次世界大戦が終結する。 World War 2 ends.	—
	1945年	米ドルが実質的な基軸通貨になる。 The U.S. dollar becomes the world key currency.	p142
	1945年〜	財閥解体が行なわれる。 The dismantling of the Zaibatsu is conducted.	p176
	1946年〜	IMF（国際通貨基金）、IBRD（国際復興開発銀行）が設立される。 The International Monetary Fund (IMF) and the International Bank for Reconstruction and Development (IBRD) are established.	p140
	1947年〜	労働3法が制定される。 The three labor laws are announced.	p176

	1946年~	農地改革が行なわれる。 The farmland reform is implemented.	p176
昭和時代 Shōwa period（1926～1989年）	1947年	復興金融公庫がつくられる。 The Reconstruction Finance Bank (RFB) is established.	p178
	1948年	GATT（関税および貿易に関する一般協定）が発足する。 The General Agreement on Tariffs and Trade (GATT) is concluded.	p134
	1948年	GHQが経済安定9原則を設ける。 The General Headquarters of the Allied Force institutes the "Nine Doctrines for Economic Security"	p178
	1949年	ドッジ・ラインが実施される。 The Dodge Line is established.	p178
	1949年	1ドル＝360円の固定為替相場が設定される。 A fixed exchange rate of 360 yen to 1 U.S. dollar is established.	p178
	1950年	朝鮮戦争が勃発する。 The Korean War breaks out.	p180
	1950年~	特需景気が起こる。 A special procurement boom occurs.	p180
	1952年	欧州石炭鉄鋼共同体が発足する。 The European Coal and Steel Community (ECSC) is established.	p156
	1955年	高度経済成長期に入る。 An era of high economic growth starts.	p180
	1960年	IDA（国際開発協会）が発足、IBRDとあわせて世界銀行と呼ばれる。 The International Development Association (IDA) is set up.The IDA and the International Bank for Reconstruction and Development (IBRD) merge and become The World Bank.	—
	1960年	ベトナム戦争が勃発する。 The Vietnam War breaks out.	p142
	1967年	欧州共同体（EC）が発足する。 The European Community（EC）is established.	—
	1967年	ASEANが発足する。 The Association of Southeast Asian Nations (ASEAN) is established.	p154
	1971年	ニクソン大統領、ドル紙幣と金との兌換停止を宣言する。 President Nixon declares an end to the direct convertibility of the dollar to gold.	p144
	1973年	先進国が変動相場制に切りかえる。 The floating rate system is used for developed countries.	p144
	1973年	第4次中東戦争が勃発する。 The Fourth Middle East War breaks out.	p182
	1973年	オイルショックが起こる。 The oil shock hits the world.	p182
	1974年	高度経済成長期が終わり、安定成長期に入る。 An era of high economic growth ends and an era of stable economic growth starts.	p182
	1975年	ベトナム戦争が終結する。 The Vietnam War ends.	—
	1975年	第1回先進国首脳会議が開催される。 The first summit conference, G6 is convened.	—
	1978年	中国で改革開放政策が始まる。 The "reform and door-opening policies" is launched in China.	p158
	1980代	米国で、「双子の赤字」が問題になる。 The "Twin Deficits" becomes a concern in the U.S.	p148
	1981年	米国でレーガノミックスが行なわれる。 Reaganomics, economic policy, is implemented in the U.S.	p148
	1985年	プラザ合意が行なわれる。 The Plaza Accord is signed.	p148
	1985年	急激な円高・ドル安になる。 The Japanese yen exchange rate falls quickly, and the U.S. dollar exchange rate rises at the same time.	p148

	1986年	バブル景気が始まる。 The "bubble economy" begins.	p148 p180
平成時代　Heisei period（1989年〜）	1989年	マルタ会談で冷戦が終結する。 The Cold War ends at the Malta Summit.	p150
	1989年	ベルリンの壁が崩壊する。 The Berlin Wall is destroyed.	—
	1991年	バブル経済が崩壊する。 The "bubble economy" collapses.	p186
	1991年	ソ連が崩壊する。 The Soviet Union collapses.	—
	1991年	銀行の不良債権が問題になる。 Bank bad loan problems occur.	p186 p188
	1995年	デフレーションに傾く。 The Japanese economy shows a trend towards deflation.	p188
	1993年	欧州連合（EU）が発足する。 The European Union (EU) is established.	p156
	1997年	大手金融機関の破綻が相次ぐ。 Several large financial institutions go bankrupt one after another.	p188
	1998年	ロシアが参加して、G8（主要国首脳会議）が開催される。 The G8 summit including Russia is held.	—
	1999年	G20（20カ国・地域財務大臣・中央銀行総裁会議）が開催される。 The G20 Finance Ministers and Central Bank Governors is held.	—
	2000年	米国、ITバブルが崩壊する。 The dot-com bubble collapses in the U.S.	p152
	2002年	ユーロの流通が始まる。 Use of the euro begins.	p156
	2005年	東アジア首脳会議（東アジアサミット）が開催される。 The East Asia Summit is held.	p154
	2007年	米国、サブプライム・ローン問題が起こる。 The subprime problem occurs in the U.S.	p152
	2007年	世界金融危機が起こる。 The world financial crisis begins.	p152
	2008年	リーマン・ブラザーズが倒産する。 Lehman Brothers goes bankrupt.	p152
	2008年	G20（20カ国・地域首脳会合）が開催される。 The G20 Summit is held.	—
	2010年	中国のGDPが世界第2位になる。 China becomes a major economic power with the second largest GDP in the world.	p158
	2011年	東日本大震災が起こる。 The Great East Japan Earthquake takes place.	p190
	2011年	31年ぶりに日本の貿易収支が赤字に転じる。 Japanesse trede balance falls into negative territory for the first time in 31 years.	—
	2012年	ギリシアで金融危機が起こる。 Greece's financial crisis occurs.	p156
	2012年	日中間に尖閣問題が起こる。 Between Japan and China, the Senkaku island issue occurs.	p156
	2013年	日銀が異次元緩和を開始。 The Bank of Japan began to implement the "different dimension" easing.	p106
	2014年	消費税を8%に増税 Consumption tax increased to 8%.	p62
令和時代	2019年	消費税を10%に増税 Consumption tax increased to 10%.	p62
	2020年	新型コロナ感染症が世界的流行。 New coronavirus infection became a global epidemic.	—

INDEX / さくいん

監 修 者

大島朋剛（おおしま　ともたか）

1976 年東京都生まれ。東京大学大学院経済学研究科博士課程修了。専門は日本経済史、日本経営史、流通史。
現在、神奈川大学経済学部准教授。共著書『国分三百年史』（2015 年）のほか、「灘酒造家による事業の多角化と資産管理－辰馬本家を事例として－」（『企業家研究』、2010 年）など日本の酒造業史に関連する論文が多数ある。

英 文 監 訳 者

Elizabeth Mills（エリザベス・ミルズ）

米国シアトル（ワシントン州）生まれ。セントラルワシントン大学卒業。セントラルキットサップスクールにて 18 年間、教師を務める。
現在、日本で生活。日本人の母とアメリカ人の父を持ち、夫はアメリカ人。日本の歴史・しきたり・文化・社会等に造詣が深い。英文監訳者として、『英語対訳で読む禅入門』、『英語対訳で読む美しい日本の「こころ」』（実業之日本社）ほかの評価が高い。

英 文 監 訳 協 力 者

Jared Kettler（ジャレッド・ケトラー）

1984 年米国ダナ・ポイント（カリフォルニア州）生まれ。チャップマン大学で MBA を取得したのち、アラスカ大学で航空学、経営学を学ぶ。現在は Accusource LLC で資産運用のスペシャリストとしてコンサルタント業務を担当している。

じっぴコンパクト新書 382

JIPPI Compact

経済の基礎も英語も学べる！
新版 英語対訳で読む「経済」入門
Introduction to the Economy

2020 年 10 月 7 日　初版第 1 刷発行

監修者 ……… **大島朋剛 + Elizabeth Mills**
発行者 ……… **岩野裕一**
発行所 ……… **株式会社 実業之日本社**
〒 107- 0062 東京都港区南青山 5-4-30
　　　　　　　CoSTUME NATIONAL Aoyama Complex 2F
電話　（編集）03-6809-0452
　　　　（販売）03-6809-0495
https://www.j-n.co.jp/

印刷・製本 ……… **大日本印刷株式会社**